Python Unleashed

Mastering the Art of Efficient Coding

James Livingston

Table of Contents

INTRODUCTION

"Python Unleashed: Mastering the Art of Efficient Coding" is an insightful and comprehensive guide designed for programmers who wish to deepen their understanding and mastery of Python, one of the most popular programming languages in the world. This book deeply delves into Python's versatile features, emphasizing efficient and effective coding practices. It is tailored for both beginners who are just starting their coding journey and experienced developers seeking to refine their skills in Python.

The book begins with an overview of Python's unique characteristics, setting it apart from other programming languages. It then progressively introduces the reader to Python's syntax and core concepts, ensuring a solid foundation. As the chapters advance, the focus shifts towards more advanced topics such as data structures, algorithms, object-oriented programming, and functional programming concepts. Each concept is explained with clear examples and practical code snippets, making the learning process engaging and interactive.

"Python Unleashed: Mastering the Art of Efficient Coding" teaches Python programming and encourages best practices in coding. It includes debugging, error handling, and performance optimization sections, which are crucial for writing clean, efficient, and maintainable code. The book is replete with real-world projects and case studies, providing readers with hands-on experience and preparing them to tackle real-life programming challenges. By the end of this book, readers will have gained a comprehensive understanding of Python and the skills to write efficient, effective, and professional-grade code.

CHAPTER I

Getting Started with Python

Setting up a Python development environment

Python, a versatile and widely used programming language, has gained immense popularity among developers for its simplicity and robustness. Whether you're a beginner taking your first steps into the world of programming or an experienced coder, setting up a Python development environment is a crucial initial step. This environment encompasses everything from the Python interpreter to code editors, libraries, and tools necessary for efficiently writing, testing, and debugging Python code. This section will delve into setting up a Python development environment, exploring the key components and considerations involved.

The fundamental component of any Python development environment is the Python interpreter itself. Python is an interpreted language, which means that code is executed line by line by the interpreter. Developers have a choice of Python versions, with Python 2.x and Python 3.x being the most prominent. As of my last knowledge update in January 2022, Python 2.x is no longer supported, and Python 3.x is the recommended version. Installing Python is usually straightforward; Python's official website provides installation packages for various operating systems. Additionally, there are package managers like Anaconda, which make it easy to manage different Python versions and libraries for data science tasks.

Once you have Python installed, the next step is selecting a code editor or integrated development environment

(IDE). Choosing the right editor is essential, as it greatly impacts your coding experience and productivity. Some popular options include Visual Studio Code, PyCharm, Sublime Text, and Jupyter Notebook. These editors offer features like syntax highlighting, code completion, and debugging tools, making them indispensable for Python development. Visual Studio Code, for instance, has gained popularity due to its extensive extension ecosystem, which allows you to customize and enhance your development environment according to your needs.

With Python installed and an editor in place, the next consideration is organizing your project structure. Proper project organization is essential for maintaining a clean and manageable codebase. Common practices include creating separate directories for source code, documentation, tests, and dependencies. This structure makes your code more maintainable and facilitates collaboration with other developers.

Python's package management system, pip, plays a vital role in managing project dependencies. You can use pip to install and manage external libraries and packages required for your projects. Additionally, Python's virtual environments enable you to isolate project-specific dependencies, preventing conflicts between different projects. Tools like virtualenv and conda are widely used for creating and managing virtual environments. This isolation ensures that your project remains self-contained and reproducible, regardless of the system it is running on.

Another crucial aspect of setting up a Python development environment is version control. Version control systems, such as Git, allow developers to track changes in their codebase, collaborate with others, and revert to previous states if needed. Platforms like GitHub and GitLab provide hosting for Git repositories, making it easier to collaborate with a team and contribute to open-source projects.

Testing is an integral part of software development, and Python offers various testing frameworks like unittest, pytest, and nose. These frameworks allow you to write and execute tests to ensure your code behaves as expected. Properly testing your code helps catch bugs early in development and ensures that new changes do not introduce regressions.

For debugging Python code, developers have access to various tools and techniques. Most Python IDEs have built-in debugging features, allowing you to set breakpoints, inspect variables, and step through your code to identify and fix issues. Additionally, you can use external tools like pdb (Python Debugger) for debugging.

Documentation is often an overlooked but critical aspect of software development. Python's built-in documentation system, based on docstrings and tools like Sphinx, allows you to create comprehensive documentation for your codebase. Well-documented code makes it easier for others (and your future self) to understand and use your code effectively.

Python's ecosystem extends beyond just code and development tools. The Python Package Index (PyPI) hosts a vast repository of open-source packages and libraries that can accelerate your development process. Whether you need web frameworks like Django or Flask, data analysis tools like pandas, or machine learning libraries like TensorFlow, PyPI has you covered.

In conclusion, setting up a Python development environment involves several key components and considerations. Starting with installing Python itself, you must choose a suitable code editor or IDE, organize your project structure, manage dependencies with pip and virtual environments, utilize version control systems like Git, incorporate testing and debugging practices, and document your code effectively. With a well-configured environment, you can harness the power of Python to tackle a wide range of projects, from web development to data science and beyond. Whether you're a novice or a seasoned developer, the right Python development environment can significantly enhance your coding experience and productivity.

Your first Python program

Programming is a powerful skill that empowers individuals to create, automate, and solve various problems. When embarking on the journey of learning programming, one of the most common starting points is Python. Python is a prevalent and beginner-friendly programming language known for its simplicity and readability. In this section, we will explore the experience of writing your first Python program, touching upon the language's fundamental concepts and the sense of accomplishment of taking those initial steps into coding.

Python's simplicity begins with its syntax. Unlike other programming languages that require intricate symbols and complex structures, Python is designed to read like plain English. This aspect of Python makes it particularly welcoming for beginners. A Python program typically starts with a simple "Hello, World!" example, where you print those words to the screen. It's a way to get familiar with the basic structure of a Python program.
print("Hello, World!")

This single line of code encapsulates the essence of Python. The print function, which is built into Python, is used to display text on the screen. In this case, it's displaying the famous greeting. This straightforwardness is one of the key reasons why Python is often recommended as a first programming language.

Another fundamental concept in Python is variables. Variables allow you to store and manipulate data. In

Python, you can declare a variable by simply assigning a value to it. For instance, let's create a variable name to store a person's name and then print a customized message.

```
name = "Alice"

print("Hello, " + name + "!")
```

Here, we assign the value "Alice" to the name variable and then use it within the print statement. Python allows you to concatenate strings (combine them) using the + operator, making creating dynamic messages easy. Control structures are another essential aspect of programming, and Python provides various ways to control the flow of your program. Conditional statements, like if, allow you to execute different code blocks based on certain conditions. For example, you can write a program that checks if a number is positive or negative and prints an appropriate message.

```
number = -5


if number > 0:

print("The number is positive.")

elif number < 0:

print("The number is negative.")

else:

print("The number is zero.")
```

In this code, we use if, elif (short for "else if"), and else to define three different scenarios based on the value of the number variable. This demonstrates how Python facilitates decision-making in your programs.

Loops are another critical concept in programming, and Python offers two primary loop structures: for and while. A for loop allows you to iterate over a sequence, such as a list or range of numbers, executing a block of code for each iteration. Here's an example of a simple for loop that counts from 1 to 5 and prints each number.

```
for i in range(1, 6):

print(i)
```

The range function generates a sequence of numbers from 1 to 5 (inclusive) that the for loop iterates through. Python's for loops are incredibly versatile and can be used for various tasks.

On the other hand, a while loop repeatedly executes a block of code as long as a certain condition is met. Here's an example of a while loop that counts from 1 to 5, similar to the previous for loop.

```
i = 1

while i <= 5:

print(i)

i += 1
```

In this code, we use the while loop to count from 1 to 5 by incrementing the i variable inside the loop. This demonstrates how Python's flexibility allows you to choose the proper loop structure for your specific needs.

In addition to these core concepts, Python also provides a vast ecosystem of libraries and modules that expand its capabilities. You can easily leverage libraries for data analysis, web development, machine learning, and more tasks. This makes Python an excellent choice for beginners and a versatile tool for experienced programmers.

As you write your first Python program and explore these fundamental concepts, you'll likely encounter challenges and errors. This is a natural part of the learning process, and debugging is a valuable skill in programming. Python provides error messages that can help you identify and fix issues in your code. You'll become a more proficient programmer by reading these messages and understanding the code.

Moreover, Python's community and online resources are invaluable when you're stuck or seeking guidance. Numerous forums, tutorials, and documentation are available to assist you on your coding journey. Don't hesitate to seek help from these resources when needed.

In conclusion, writing your first Python program is a significant milestone in your programming journey. Python's simplicity, readability, and versatility make it an excellent choice for beginners. As you learn the fundamental concepts of Python, such as syntax, variables, control structures, and loops, you'll gain the confidence and skills to tackle more complex programming challenges. Embrace the learning and problem-solving process, and you'll find that programming with Python can be rewarding and enjoyable experience. So go ahead, start coding, and discover the endless possibilities that await you in the world of Python programming.

Understanding Python's syntax and data types

Python is a versatile and powerful programming language known for its simplicity and readability. One of the fundamental aspects of Python that every programmer should grasp is its syntax and data types. Python's syntax, characterized by its clean and straightforward structure and diverse data types, plays a pivotal role in making it a preferred choice for both beginners and experienced developers.

At the heart of Python's appeal is its elegant and human-readable syntax. Unlike many other programming languages, Python emphasizes code readability by employing indentation instead of traditional braces or brackets. This indentation-based approach forces developers to write clean and organized code, making it easier for them to understand and collaborate on projects. Python's commitment to readability is evident in the famous "Zen of Python," a collection of guiding principles for writing computer programs in the language. Among these principles is the belief that "Readability counts," highlighting the language's strong emphasis on code clarity.

Python's syntax is also characterized by its simplicity and minimalism. Developers often find Python code concise and expressive, meaning they can accomplish more with fewer lines of code than other languages. For instance, Python uses a straightforward and intuitive syntax for variable assignment, such as "x = 10" to assign the value 10 to the variable x. This simplicity extends to basic arithmetic operations, making writing and understanding mathematical expressions easy. Python's syntax prioritizes ease of use, making it an ideal choice for beginners looking to enter the programming world.

Python's data types are another crucial aspect that programmers must grasp to work with the language effectively. Python provides a variety of data types that allow developers to store and manipulate different kinds of information. One of Python's most basic data types is the integer (int). Integers are whole numbers and can be used for tasks like counting, indexing, or representing quantities. Python also supports floating-point numbers (float), which include decimal values and are suitable for more precise calculations. Strings (str) are used to represent text and are essential for handling textual data in Python programs.

Lists and tuples are two essential data types in Python for storing collections of items. Lists are mutable, which means you can modify their contents after creation, making them suitable for tasks like dynamic data storage. Conversely, Tuples are immutable, making them ideal for situations where data should remain unchanged. Both lists and tuples allow you to store a mix of data types, offering flexibility in data manipulation. Dictionaries (dict) are Python's way of implementing key-value pairs, allowing efficient data retrieval based on keys. This data type is valuable for organizing and accessing data quickly.

Python also includes sets (set) and frozen sets (frozenset) for handling unique collections of items. Sets automatically remove duplicate elements, while frozen sets are immutable, ensuring their contents remain constant. These data types are valuable when working with mathematical sets or when you need to eliminate duplicates from a collection.

Understanding Python's data types also involves exploring the concept of typecasting. Typecasting allows you to convert data from one type to another, which can be useful when performing various operations. Python provides built-in functions for typecasting, such as int(), float(), and str(), making it easy to switch between data types when needed.

In addition to the built-in data types, Python allows developers to create custom data types through classes. Classes define the structure and behavior of objects, enabling developers to model real-world entities and implement complex data structures. This object-oriented approach enhances code organization and encapsulation, contributing to the maintainability and scalability of Python programs.

Python's dynamic typing system is another crucial aspect to understand when working with data types. Unlike statically typed languages that require explicit data type declarations, Python infers the data type of a variable at runtime. This dynamic typing simplifies code writing but demands a clear understanding of the data being manipulated to avoid unexpected errors. Python's flexibility and dynamic typing enable rapid development and experimentation, as developers can change variable types as needed during program execution.

To effectively work with Python's syntax and data types, it is essential to have a solid grasp of conditional statements, loops, and functions. Conditional statements, including if, elif, and else, allow you to control the flow of your program based on certain conditions. Loops like for and while enable you to iterate through collections or repeat actions until a specified condition is met. Functions are reusable blocks of code that encapsulate specific functionality, promoting modularity and code reusability.

In conclusion, understanding Python's syntax and data types is essential for novice and experienced programmers. Python's clean and readable syntax encourages good coding practices, while its diverse data types provide flexibility and power in handling different data types. Whether you are just starting your programming journey or are an experienced developer, a solid understanding of Python's syntax and data types is the foundation for writing efficient and maintainable code in this popular and versatile programming language.

CHAPTER II

Variables, Data Structures, and Operators

Working with variables and data types

Python, a versatile and widely used programming language, owes much of its popularity to its simplicity and flexibility. One of the fundamental concepts in Python programming is the manipulation of variables and data types. Variables serve as containers for storing and managing data, while data types define the kind of data that variables can hold. A solid understanding of how to work with variables and data types is essential for any Python programmer, from beginners taking their first steps in programming to experienced developers tackling complex projects.

Variables in Python are like named storage locations that allow you to store and retrieve data. Unlike other programming languages, Python is dynamically typed, meaning you don't need to declare a variable's data type explicitly. When you assign a value to a variable, Python automatically determines its data type based on the given value. For example, if you set the value 10 to a variable named x, Python understands that x is an integer.

The naming of variables in Python follows a set of rules. Variable names can consist of letters, numbers, and underscores, but they must start with a letter or an underscore. They are case-sensitive, so myVar and myvar are considered two different variables. Additionally, Python has reserved words, known as keywords, that cannot be used as variable names because they have special meanings in the language. For instance, you cannot name a variable "if" or "while" because these are keywords used for control flow.

Python offers a variety of data types to accommodate different kinds of data. The fundamental data types in Python include integers (int), floating-point numbers (float), and strings (str). Integers are used to represent whole numbers, while floating-point numbers handle decimal values with precision. Strings are employed for textual data, and they can be enclosed in either single (' ') or double (" ") quotes. For instance, you can declare a variable name and assign it the string value "John."

Lists and tuples are two crucial data types for managing collections of items. Square brackets denote lists and can contain various data types, making them versatile for various purposes. You can change a list's contents after creation, making them mutable. Conversely, Tuples use parentheses and are immutable, meaning their elements cannot be modified once defined. This immutability ensures the data remains constant throughout the program.

Dictionaries (dict) are key-value pairs that allow you to associate values with unique keys. They are essential for efficient data retrieval and organization. Each key in a dictionary maps to a specific value, enabling fast lookups. For example, you can create a dictionary to store the age of individuals using their names as keys.

Sets and frozen sets are used to handle unique collections of items. Sets automatically remove duplicate elements, ensuring that each item is unique within the set. Frozen sets are similar but are immutable, making them useful for situations where you want to ensure that the data remains unchanged.

Python also provides mechanisms for typecasting, allowing you to convert data from one type to another. For example, you can convert an integer to a floating- point number using the float() function or a floating-point number to an integer with the int() function. Typecasting is a valuable tool when you need to perform operations that involve different data types.

Working with variables and data types also involves understanding operators, which are symbols or words that perform operations on data. Python supports a wide range of operators, including arithmetic operators (+, -, *, /, %), comparison operators (==, !=, <, >, <=, >=), and logical operators (and, or, not). These operators allow you to perform calculations, compare, and implement logical conditions in your code.

Variable scope is another critical aspect to consider when working with variables. In Python, the scope of a variable determines where it can be accessed and modified. Variables can have local or global scope. A local variable is defined within a specific function or block of code and is accessible only within that scope. Global variables, on the other hand, are defined outside of any function and can be accessed from anywhere in the program.

Understanding variable scope is crucial for avoiding naming conflicts and managing data effectively in your programs.

Furthermore, Python's dynamic typing system enables you to change the type of a variable during program execution. While this flexibility is a strength of Python, it can also lead to unexpected errors if not managed carefully. It is essential to be aware of the data type of a variable at any given time and use typecasting when necessary to ensure consistent data manipulation.

In conclusion, working with variables and data types is a fundamental skill for Python programmers. Variables are containers that hold data, and data types define the kind of data that variables can store. Python's dynamic typing system and extensive set of built-in data types make it a flexible and powerful language for various applications. Whether you are a beginner or an experienced developer, mastering the concepts of variables and data types in Python is essential for writing efficient and effective code.

Exploring Python's built-in data structures

Python, a widely-used and versatile programming language, offers a rich set of built-in data structures that are essential for manipulating and organizing data efficiently. These data structures are fundamental components of Python programming and play a crucial role in developing robust and efficient applications. Understanding and mastering these data structures is a key step toward becoming a proficient Python programmer.

The list is one of the most commonly used built-in data structures in Python. A list is an ordered collection of items that can store elements of different data types. Lists are defined using square brackets and can contain any combination of integers, floating-point numbers, strings, and even other lists. Lists are mutable, meaning you can modify their contents by adding, removing, or updating elements. This flexibility makes lists versatile and suitable for a wide range of tasks, from storing a list of names to representing a sequence of numbers for mathematical calculations.

Another essential data structure in Python is the tuple. Tuples are similar to lists in that they can store a collection of items but differ in one critical aspect: tuples are immutable. Once you create a tuple and assign its values, you cannot change those values. Tuples are defined using parentheses and often represent data that should remain constant throughout the program's execution. For example, you might use a tuple to store the coordinates of a fixed point in a 2D space.

Dictionaries are Python's solution for implementing key-value pairs. A dictionary, denoted by curly braces {}, allows you to associate unique keys with corresponding values. This data structure provides fast and efficient data retrieval based on keys. Dictionaries are incredibly versatile and can store data of various types as values, including lists, tuples, and even other dictionaries. They are particularly useful for tasks that involve mapping between items, such as storing data related to individuals with their names as keys and corresponding information as values.

Sets and frozen sets are data structures used to handle collections of unique items. Sets are defined using curly braces {} and automatically remove duplicate elements, ensuring each item in the set is unique. They are mutable, allowing you to add or remove elements as needed. On the other hand, frozen sets are similar to sets but are immutable, making them suitable for situations where you want to ensure that the data remains constant throughout the program. Sets are valuable for various applications, such as finding unique values in a list or checking for membership in a collection.

Python also includes a built-in data structure called the deque, short for "double-ended queue." A deque is a versatile and efficient data structure that allows you to add and remove elements from both ends of the collection with constant time complexity. This makes it an excellent choice for implementing queues and stacks, which are essential in many algorithms and data processing scenarios. Deques can be created using the collections module in Python.

Furthermore, Python provides two data structures for representing ordered collections: the list and the tuple. Both lists and tuples maintain the order of their elements, allowing you to access and iterate through them predictably. Lists are mutable, which means you can change their contents after creation. In contrast, tuples are immutable, ensuring that their elements remain constant. Depending on the requirements of your program, you can choose between lists and tuples to store ordered data collections.

Python's built-in data structures are not only diverse but also highly efficient. They have been designed and optimized to perform well in various scenarios, making them suitable for both small-scale scripts and large-scale applications. Understanding when and how to use each data structure is crucial for writing efficient and maintainable Python code.

In addition to the core built-in data structures mentioned above, Python also provides a wide range of additional data structures through various libraries and modules. For instance, the collections module offers specialized data structures like namedtuples, defaultdicts, and OrderedDicts, which can be incredibly useful for specific tasks. Similarly, the heapq module provides functions for working with heaps, a type of binary tree used in priority queues and other data manipulation scenarios.

In conclusion, exploring Python's built-in data structures is fundamental in becoming proficient in the language. These data structures, including lists, tuples, dictionaries, sets, and deques, provide versatile and efficient tools for managing and organizing data in Python programs. Mastering these data structures and understanding their characteristics and use cases are essential skills for any Python programmer, as they enable you to write more efficient, readable, and maintainable code for a wide range of applications.

Using operators for calculations and comparisons

Python, a versatile and widely-used programming language, provides a variety of operators that enable programmers to perform calculations and comparisons on data. These operators are fundamental to writing effective Python code, whether you're working on simple mathematical calculations or complex logical evaluations. Understanding how to use operators in Python is crucial for any programmer.

Arithmetic operators are one of the most basic sets of operators in Python. These operators allow you to perform basic mathematical operations such as addition (+), subtraction (-), multiplication (*), division (/), and modulus (%). The modulus operator returns the remainder of a division operation, which is particularly useful when dealing with repeating patterns or cyclic data. For example, you can use the modulus operator to check if a number is even or odd by dividing it by 2 and examining the remainder.

Comparison operators in Python enable you to compare values and expressions, producing Boolean results (True or False). These operators include equality (==), inequality (!=), less than (<), greater than (>), less than or equal to (<=), and greater than or equal to (>=). Comparison operators are essential for making decisions in your code based on conditions. For instance, you can use the equality operator to check if two values are equal, and you can use the greater than operator to determine if one value is larger than another.

Logical operators are used to perform logical operations on Boolean values or expressions. Python provides three main logical operators: and, or, and not.
The and operator returns True if both operands are True, the or operator returns True if at least one operand is True, and the not operator negates the value of the

operand, turning True into False and vice versa. Logical operators are crucial for building complex decision-making structures in your code and for evaluating multiple conditions simultaneously.

In addition to these fundamental operators, Python also offers assignment operators, which allow you to assign values to variables in a concise manner while performing an operation. For example, the += operator adds the value on the right side to the variable on the left side and assigns the result back to the variable. This is useful for incrementing variables or accumulating values over time. Other assignment operators include -=, *=, /=, and %=, each corresponding to a specific operation.

Bitwise operators are a more specialized set of operators that operate on individual bits of binary representations of values. These operators include bitwise AND (&), bitwise OR (|), bitwise XOR (^), bitwise NOT (~), left shift (<<), and right shift (>>). While bitwise operators are not commonly used in everyday programming, they are essential in specific low-level or hardware-related tasks where bit-level manipulation is necessary.

Another critical group of operators in Python is the membership operators. These operators, in and not in, are used to test if a value is present in a sequence, such as a list, tuple, string, or set. For example, you can use the in operator to check if a specific element exists in a list, and the not in operator to determine if an element is absent.

The identity operators, is and is not, are used to compare the identity of objects rather than their values. Two objects with the same value may not necessarily be the same object in memory. The is operator checks if two variables refer to the same object, while the is not operator checks if they do not. These operators are beneficial when working with mutable objects like lists and dictionaries.

Conditional expressions, also known as ternary operators, concisely perform conditional assignments in Python. The conditional expression takes the form value_if_true if condition else value_if_false. It allows you to assign different values to a variable based on whether a condition is True or False. For example, you can use a conditional expression to assign a message to a variable based on whether a specific condition is met.

In Python, you can also perform string concatenation using the + operator. This operator allows you to combine two or more strings into a single string. For example, you can concatenate first and last names to create an entire name string. Additionally, you can repeat a string multiple times using the * operator. This can be useful when you need to generate repetitive patterns or formatting.

Understanding operator precedence is crucial when using multiple operators in a single expression. Operator precedence determines the order in which operators are evaluated within an expression. Python follows a well-defined operator precedence hierarchy, where certain operators are evaluated before others. For example, multiplication (*) and division (/) have higher precedence than addition (+) and subtraction (-). Parentheses can be used to override the default precedence and control the order of evaluation.

In conclusion, operators are fundamental tools in Python for performing calculations and making comparisons. Whether you are working with arithmetic operations, logical evaluations, assignments, or other tasks, understanding how to use operators effectively is essential for writing clear, concise, and efficient Python code. Mastery of operators enables you to manipulate data, make decisions, and control the flow of your programs, making you a more proficient Python programmer.

CHAPTER III

Control Flow and Loops

Conditional statements and decision-making in Python

Conditional statements are an essential aspect of programming in Python, enabling developers to make decisions and control their code flow. In Python, as in many programming languages, conditional statements allow you to execute specific code blocks based on certain conditions or criteria. Understanding how to use conditional statements effectively is fundamental for writing robust and dynamic Python programs.

The most basic conditional statement in Python is the "if" statement. An "if" statement is used to execute a block of code only if a specified condition is true. The condition is evaluated as either true or false, and the code within the "if" block is executed if the condition is evaluated to be true. If the condition is false, the code within the "if" block is skipped, and program execution continues with the next statement after the "if" block. For example, you can use an "if" statement to check if a user's age is greater than or equal to 18 before allowing them access to a restricted area of your program.

Python also provides the "else" statement, which is often used in conjunction with "if" statements to give an alternative block of code to execute when the condition in the "if" statement is evaluated to be false. The "else" block is executed if and only if the condition in the preceding "if" statement is false. This allows you to define specific behavior for cases where the condition is not met. For example, you can use an "if-else" statement to determine whether a user is eligible for a discount based on their membership status.

In addition to "if" and "else," Python offers the "elif" statement, short for "else if." The "elif" statement allows you to specify multiple conditions and associated code blocks, providing a way to test multiple conditions in sequence. When the "if" condition is false, the program evaluates the first "elif" condition. If the first "elif" condition is true, the code block associated with it is executed, and subsequent "elif" conditions are skipped.

This continues until either one of the conditions evaluates to true, in which case its associated code block is executed, or all conditions are false, in which case the code block within the "else" statement (if present) is executed. The "elif" statement is invaluable for handling complex decision-making scenarios in your code.

Python's conditional statements also support nested structures, where one conditional statement is placed inside another. This allows you to create more intricate decision trees by combining multiple "if," "elif," and "else" statements. For example, you can use nested conditional statements to implement a grading system that considers the numeric score and the grading scale to assign student letter grades.

In addition to the basic conditional statements, Python provides a shorthand known as the ternary conditional expression. This expression allows you to execute different code blocks based on a condition in a single line of code. The ternary conditional expression takes the form value_if_true if condition else value_if_false. It evaluates the condition and returns value_if_true if the condition is true or value_if_false if the condition is false. The ternary conditional expression is a concise way to make decisions in your code and assign different values to a variable based on a condition.

Python also offers the "pass" statement, which is a placeholder statement that does nothing. It is often used when you need to include a block of code for syntactical reasons but don't want the code to perform any specific actions. For example, you might use the "pass" statement as a placeholder in an empty function or an empty "if" block while you are developing your code.

Conditional statements in Python can be enhanced with logical operators that allow you to combine multiple conditions to create more complex decision-making logic. Python provides three main logical operators: "and," "or," and "not." The "and" operator returns true if both operands are true, the "or" operator returns true if at least one operand is true, and the "not" operator negates the value of the operand, turning true into false and vice versa. These logical operators are useful for creating conditions that depend on the conjunction or disjunction of multiple criteria.

Moreover, conditional statements can be used to control the flow of loops. Python provides the "break" and "continue" statements, which allow you to manipulate the execution of loops based on conditions. The "break" statement is used to exit a loop prematurely when a specific condition is met. This is useful when you want to terminate a loop when a specific event occurs. On the other hand, the "continue" statement allows you to skip the rest of the current iteration of a loop and proceed to the next iteration based on a condition. This is helpful when skipping certain elements or values during iteration.

In conclusion, conditional statements are fundamental for making decisions and controlling the flow of Python programs. Whether you are using "if," "else," "elif," nested structures, or the ternary conditional expression, understanding how to employ these statements effectively is essential for writing dynamic and responsive code. Conditional statements provide the flexibility needed to handle a wide range of decision-making scenarios in your Python programs, making them a fundamental concept for any Python programmer to master.

Loops and iteration techniques

Python, a high-level and versatile programming language, provides various mechanisms for repetitive tasks, known as loops and iteration techniques. These powerful constructs play a fundamental role in programming by allowing developers to execute a code block repeatedly until a specific condition is met. In Python, there are two primary loops: "for" loops and "while" loops, each serving distinct purposes and offering different ways to implement iterative solutions.

The "for" loop is a commonly used iteration technique in Python. It is beneficial when you have a known number of iterations or when you want to iterate over elements in a collection, such as lists, tuples, or strings. The basic syntax of a "for" loop consists of the "for" keyword, a loop variable, the "in" keyword, and an iterable object. For example, to iterate through a list of numbers and print each one, you can use a "for" loop as follows:
numbers = [1, 2, 3, 4, 5]

for num in numbers:

print(num)

In this example, the loop variable "num" takes on the values from the "numbers" list in each iteration, and the code block indented under the "for" statement is executed. The output will be each number from the list printed one by one.

Python also provides a useful function called "range()" that generates a sequence of numbers, making it convenient for iterating a specific number of times. For instance, if you want to perform a task ten times, you can use a "for" loop with the "range()" function like this:

```python
for i in range(10):

print("Iteration", i + 1)
```

This code snippet will print the message "Iteration" followed by the inclusive numbers from 1 to 10.
In contrast, the "while" loop in Python is used when the number of iterations is not known in advance but depends on a particular condition. The "while" loop repeatedly executes a code block as long as a specified condition remains true. For example, let's create a "while" loop that counts down from 5 to 1:

```python
count = 5

while count > 0:

print(count)

count -= 1
```

In this case, the loop continues until the "count" variable becomes less than or equal to 0. It decrements the "count" by 1 in each iteration and prints the current value.

To further enhance the functionality of loops, Python provides control statements like "break" and "continue." The "break" statement allows you to exit a loop prematurely if a specific condition is met. Consider the following example, where we use a "for" loop to find the first even number in a list:

```python
numbers = [1, 3, 5, 8, 10, 11, 12]

for num in numbers:
```

```python
if num % 2 == 0:

    print("First even number:", num)

    break
```

In this case, the loop stops as soon as an even number is found, and the first even number encountered is printed. Conversely, the "continue" statement skips the current iteration of a loop when a particular condition is met but allows the loop to continue with the next iteration. Here's an example that demonstrates the use of "continue" in a "for" loop to print all odd numbers in a list:

```python
numbers = [1, 3, 5, 8, 10, 11, 12]

for num in numbers:

    if num % 2 == 0:

        continue

    print("Odd number:", num)
```

The "continue" statement skips the even numbers in this code and only prints the odd ones.

Additionally, Python introduces the concept of nested loops, where one loop is placed inside another. This allows for more complex iterations. Consider a scenario where you need to print all possible combinations of two dice rolls:

```python
for die1 in range(1, 7):

    for die2 in range(1, 7):

        print("Die 1:", die1, "Die 2:", die2)
```

Nested loops are valuable for solving problems that involve multiple levels of iteration or for iterating through multi-dimensional data structures like lists of lists.

In conclusion, loops and iteration techniques are fundamental components of Python programming. "For" loops are excellent for iterating over known collections or a specified number of times, while "while" loops are suitable when you need to repeat a task until a specific condition is met. Control statements like "break" and "continue" provide fine-grained control over loop execution, and the concept of nested loops allows you to tackle complex iterative tasks effectively. Mastery of these loop constructs empowers Python developers to write efficient and flexible code to solve a wide range of problems.

Best practices for writing clean and readable code

Python is renowned for its simplicity and readability, making it a favorite language for beginners and experienced developers. However, writing clean and readable code in Python is not automatic; it requires adherence to best practices and coding conventions. In this section, we will explore the essential principles and guidelines that can help developers produce code that is not only functional but also maintainable and understandable.

One of the fundamental principles in writing clean Python code is adhering to the PEP 8 style guide. PEP 8, short for "Python Enhancement Proposal 8," is the official style guide for Python code. It provides recommendations on everything from naming conventions to indentation, ensuring that Python code looks consistent and is easy to read across different projects and by different developers. By following PEP 8, you ensure that your codebase remains coherent, making it easier for others to understand and collaborate on your code.

Meaningful variable and function names are crucial for code readability. When naming variables, functions, and classes, use descriptive names that convey their purpose.

For example, instead of naming a variable "x" or "temp," use a more descriptive name like "total_sales" or "user_input." Similarly, when defining functions or methods, choose names that clearly indicate their functionality, making it easier for others (and your future self) to understand what the code does without diving into the implementation details.

Another best practice is to keep your code concise and modular. Functions and classes should have a single, well-defined responsibility. This concept, known as the Single Responsibility Principle, helps create code that is easier to understand and maintain. Avoid writing overly long functions or classes that try to do too much. Break down complex tasks into smaller, reusable functions, and then compose them to achieve your desired functionality. This promotes code reusability and makes it more readable by abstracting away intricate details.

Proper indentation and formatting are crucial for code readability in Python. Python uses indentation to signify code blocks, so consistent and appropriate indentation is essential. PEP 8 recommends using four spaces for indentation. Additionally, you should use blank lines to separate different sections of your code, such as functions, classes, and logical blocks. Clear and consistent formatting enhances code comprehension and makes it easier to spot errors or issues.

Commenting and documentation are vital aspects of writing clean and readable code. While Python's readability often minimizes the need for excessive comments, it's still essential to include comments where necessary to explain complex algorithms, non-obvious decisions, or the purpose of specific code blocks. Use docstrings to document functions, classes, and modules, following the conventions outlined in PEP 257. Well-documented code not only aids in understanding but also simplifies the process of maintaining and updating codebases over time.

Consistency is key in writing clean Python code. Adhering to consistent coding conventions throughout your project helps prevent confusion and enhances code readability. This consistency encompasses various aspects, such as naming conventions, style, and the use of language features. Adhering to agreed-upon coding standards becomes even more crucial when collaborating with others on a project.

Another aspect to consider is the use of meaningful comments and docstrings. While Python's clean and readable syntax often reduces the need for excessive commenting, there are situations where adding comments is essential. Comments should provide valuable context, explaining why certain decisions were made or how a complex algorithm works. However, avoid over-commenting, as this can clutter the code and make it harder to read.

Efficiently managing imports is essential for code clarity and maintainability. PEP 8 recommends organizing imports in a specific order, with standard library imports first, followed by third-party library imports, and finally, local module imports. Additionally, use clear and concise aliases for modules or objects when importing to avoid confusion. For instance, instead of importing a module as "my_module," use an alias like "import my_module as mm" if it significantly improves code readability.

Effective use of white space can significantly enhance code readability. Use blank lines to separate different sections of your code, such as functions, classes, or logical blocks. Properly spacing out code improves visual separation and helps readers focus on one section at a time. Additionally, avoid excessively long lines of code, which can be challenging to read. Break long lines into multiple lines with appropriate indentation for better readability.

Python's dynamic typing can be a blessing and a curse regarding code readability. While Python's flexibility allows you to write concise code, it can also lead to confusion if variable types are unclear. To mitigate this, use meaningful variable names that indicate their purpose and, when necessary, provide type hints using Python's type hinting system. Type hints clarify the expected types of variables and function arguments, making the code more understandable and self-documenting.

When writing conditional statements, strive for clarity and simplicity. Avoid complex nested conditions that can be challenging to follow. Instead, use meaningful comparison operators to break down complex conditions into smaller, well-named variables or functions. Additionally, consider using the "elif" clause when dealing with multiple conditions to improve readability and maintainability.

Exception handling is a crucial aspect of writing robust Python code, but it should also be done with clarity in mind. Use try-except blocks to handle exceptions gracefully, and only catch specific exceptions that you expect to occur. Avoid broad exception handlers that catch all exceptions, as they can hide errors and make debugging difficult. Include meaningful error messages or comments in your exception handling code to provide context about what went wrong and why.

In conclusion, writing clean and readable code in Python is about functionality and fostering maintainability, collaboration, and long-term viability. Adhering to coding conventions like PEP 8, using meaningful names, modularizing your code, and providing clear documentation and comments are critical practices for achieving code clarity. Proper indentation, consistent formatting, and effective import management also contribute to code readability. By following these best practices, you can create Python code that is not only functional but also a pleasure to read and work with, ultimately benefiting both yourself and your collaborators.

CHAPTER IV

Functions and Modules

Defining and using functions in Python

Functions are a fundamental building block of any programming language, and Python is no exception. In Python, a function is a reusable block of code that performs a specific task or set of tasks. Functions are crucial in promoting code reusability, modularity, and readability. In this section, we will explore the concept of defining and using functions in Python, discussing their syntax, purpose, and best practices.

To define a function in Python, you use the "def" keyword followed by the function name and a pair of parentheses. Inside the parentheses, you can specify parameters, which are placeholders for values that the function will receive when called. These parameters are essential for passing information to the function. For example, here is a simple function that adds two numbers:

```
def add_numbers(x, y):

result = x + y

return result
```

In this example, the function "add_numbers" takes two parameters, "x" and "y," and calculates their sum. The "return" statement is used to specify the value that the function will return to the caller.

To use a function in Python, you call it by its name, providing arguments (values) for the parameters it expects. Using our "add_numbers" function:

result = add_numbers(3, 5)

print(result)

In this code, we call the "add_numbers" function with arguments 3 and 5, and the result is stored in the "result" variable. The "print" statement displays the value of "result," which is 8 in this case.

Functions can have multiple parameters, and they can return values or perform tasks without returning anything. For instance, consider a function that calculates the area of a rectangle:

def calculate_rectangle_area(length, width):

area = length * width

return area

This function takes two parameters, "length" and "width," and returns the calculated area. To use it:

area = calculate_rectangle_area(4, 5)

print("The area of the rectangle is:", area)

Functions in Python can also have default values for parameters. This means that if a value is not provided for a parameter when calling the function, the default value will be used instead. Here's an example:

def greet(name="Guest"):

print("Hello, " + name + "!")

In this function, "name" is a parameter with a default value of "Guest." If no name is provided when calling the function, it will greet the guest. However, you can still provide a different name if desired:

greet() # Output: Hello, Guest!

greet("Alice") # Output: Hello, Alice!

Functions can also accept a variable number of arguments using the *args and **kwargs syntax. *args allows a function to accept a variable number of positional arguments, while **kwargs allows it to accept a variable number of keyword arguments. This flexibility is useful when you don't know in advance how many arguments you'll need. Here's an example:

```python
def add(*args):

result = 0

for num in args:

result += num

return result


total = add(1, 2, 3, 4, 5)

print("Total:", total)
```

In this case, the add function can take any number of arguments, and it calculates their sum.

When writing clean and readable functions in Python, adhering to naming conventions and providing meaningful documentation is crucial. Function names should be descriptive and follow the snake_case naming convention (all lowercase with underscores separating words). Additionally, using docstrings to document your functions and clearly explain their purpose and parameters enhances code readability and helps other developers (or your future self) understand how to use them.

Functions should also adhere to the Single Responsibility Principle, which means they should have a clear and specific purpose. Functions that perform too many unrelated tasks become hard to understand and maintain. Keeping functions focused on a single responsibility improves code modularity and makes it easier to troubleshoot and update.

To ensure that functions are self-contained and do not rely on external variables, it's best practice to avoid using global variables within a function. Instead, pass any required values as parameters to the function, making it clear where the data comes from and improving code predictability.

Another best practice is to use meaningful variable names within functions, just as you would in the rest of your code. Descriptive variable names make it easier to understand the logic within the function, reducing the need for excessive comments.

In Python, functions are first-class objects, which means you can assign them to variables, pass them as arguments to other functions, and return them from other functions. This feature allows for advanced programming techniques like function decorators and higher-order functions, enhancing code modularity and maintainability.

In conclusion, defining and using functions is a fundamental aspect of Python programming. Functions encapsulate specific tasks or logic, promoting code reusability, modularity, and readability. When describing functions, adhere to naming conventions, provide meaningful documentation, and follow best practices to ensure your code is clean and maintainable. Functions allow you to break down complex tasks into manageable parts, making your code more organized and easier to understand. By mastering the art of defining and using functions in Python, you can write efficient, modular, and readable code that is both developer-friendly and maintainable in the long run.

Organizing code with modules

Python is a versatile and widely used programming language known for its simplicity and readability. As projects grow in complexity, it becomes essential to maintain a well-structured and organized codebase to ensure maintainability and ease of collaboration. One of the fundamental tools in Python for achieving code organization is using modules. Modules provide a way to encapsulate code into separate files, making it easier to manage, reuse, and maintain. In this section, we will explore the concept of modules in Python and discuss their significance in organizing code effectively.

To begin with, modules in Python are simply Python files with a .py extension that contain variables, functions, and classes. These files serve as containers for related pieces of code, allowing developers to break down their programs into smaller, manageable units. This modular approach offers several benefits. First and foremost, it enhances code readability by providing a structured way to organize code. Each module can focus on a specific aspect of the program, making it easier for developers to understand and maintain the codebase.

Moreover, modules promote code reusability. By defining functions and classes within modules, developers can reuse these components in different parts of their program or even in entirely separate projects. This reusability saves time and encourages best practices by allowing developers to write and test code once and then apply it across multiple contexts. It also fosters collaboration, as different team members can work on individual modules independently, reducing the chances of conflicts when merging code.

Python offers a straightforward way to import and use modules in a program. The import statement is used to load modules into the current script, making their contents available for use. For instance, if we have a module named math_operations.py containing various mathematical functions, we can import it into our main script as follows: import math_operations. Once imported, we can access the functions within the module using dot notation, like math_operations.add(2, 3). Python

also supports more advanced module organization through the use of packages. Packages are directories that contain multiple modules and a special __init__.py file, which indicates that the directory should be treated as a package. This hierarchical organization allows developers to group related modules together in a structured manner. Packages are beneficial when working on larger projects where the codebase can become extensive and complex.

One key advantage of packages is that they enable the creation of namespaces. A namespace is a container for identifiers (e.g., variable names, function names, and class names) that helps prevent naming conflicts between different modules. By organizing code into packages, developers can use unique names within each package without worrying about clashes with identifiers in other program parts.

Another significant feature of Python modules is the ability to include a special block of code at the end of a module that runs only when the module is executed directly, not when it's imported as a module into another script. This behavior is achieved using the if __name__ == "__main__": block. It allows developers to write code that serves as both a reusable module and a standalone script. For example, a module containing utility functions can be used by other scripts but can also be executed directly to perform specific tasks when needed.

In addition to improving code organization and promoting reusability, modules also contribute to code maintainability. When a bug or issue arises, developers can focus on the specific module or package where the problem occurs, rather than searching through a monolithic codebase. This pinpoint approach simplifies debugging and reduces the chances of introducing unintended side effects when making changes.

Furthermore, modules support version control and collaboration. By breaking down a project into smaller, manageable units, teams can work on different modules concurrently, facilitating parallel development. Version control systems like Git can track changes to individual modules, making reviewing and merging contributions from multiple team members easier.

In conclusion, organizing code with modules in Python is a fundamental practice that enhances code readability, reusability, and maintainability. Modules allow developers to encapsulate related pieces of code into separate files, making it easier to manage and understand complex programs. Developers can reuse code efficiently by importing modules, promoting best practices and collaboration. Packages extend this organization to a higher level, enabling the hierarchical structuring of modules and preventing naming conflicts. Python's support for executable scripts within modules further enhances code flexibility. Modules are an indispensable tool in Python development, essential for managing and scaling projects of any size and complexity.

Understanding scope and namespaces

Python, a popular and versatile programming language, is known for its readability and ease of use. To become proficient in Python and write effective code, it is essential to understand two fundamental concepts: scope and namespaces. Scope refers to the visibility and accessibility of variables, while namespaces are containers that hold variables, functions, and objects. In this section, we will delve into the intricacies of scope and namespaces in Python, exploring their significance in writing clean and organized code.

Python employs a hierarchical structure to manage the scope of variables. At the highest level, we have the global scope, which encompasses variables accessible throughout the entire program. Variables defined in the worldwide scope are known as global variables. These variables are typically declared outside of any function or class, making them accessible from any part of the code.

In contrast, functions and classes in Python have their own local scopes. Variables declared within these blocks are called local variables. Local variables are only accessible within the function or class in which they are defined. This encapsulation helps prevent naming conflicts and allows for the reuse of variable names in different parts of the program.

Understanding the concept of scope is crucial for writing maintainable and error-free code. When referenced, Python first searches for a variable within the current local scope. If it is not found, Python then looks in the enclosing (higher) scopes, working its way up to the global scope. This search process is known as the "LEGB" rule, which stands for Local, Enclosing, Global, and Built-in. If the variable is not found in any of these scopes, Python raises a NameError.

Namespaces play a vital role in organizing and managing variables in Python. A namespace is a mapping of variable names to objects, and it serves as a container for these names. Python has several types of namespaces, including the global namespace and local namespaces associated with functions and classes. Each module also has its own namespace, allowing variables, functions, and classes to be organized and isolated.

To further illustrate the concept of namespaces, consider the following example:

```python
x = 10 # Global variable


def my_function():

y = 20

# Local variable

print(x)

# Accessing the global variable


my_function()
```

In this example, x is defined in the global namespace, and y is defined in the local namespace of the my_function function. When we call my_function(), it can access and print the global variable x because global variables are accessible from within local scopes. However, if we attempted to print y outside of the my_function scope, we would encounter a NameError because y is not defined in the global scope.

Python also provides a built-in namespace, which contains a set of predefined functions, classes, and objects that are always available for use. These built-in functions include print(), len(), and type(), among others. Since the built-in namespace is automatically available, you can use these functions without importing any modules.

In addition to global, local, and built-in namespaces, Python allows for creating custom namespaces through modules and packages. Modules are Python files that can contain variables, functions, and classes. When a module is imported, its namespace becomes available for use in the importing script. This modular approach helps organize code by encapsulating related functionality in separate files, preventing naming conflicts, and promoting code reuse.

On the other hand, packages are directories containing multiple modules, each with its own namespace. The __init__.py file within a package directory signals that the directory should be treated as a package, allowing you to hierarchize related modules. This enables developers to create a structured and organized codebase, especially in large projects involving multiple modules.

Understanding scope and namespaces in Python is fundamental to writing clean, organized, and maintainable code. By grasping the concept of scope, developers can control the visibility and accessibility of variables, preventing unintended side effects and conflicts. Namespaces provide a systematic way to manage variables, functions, and classes, allowing for encapsulation and isolation of code elements. Whether working with global, local, built-in, or custom namespaces, Python's clear and hierarchical approach to scope and namespaces is a powerful tool for writing effective and reliable code.

CHAPTER V

Object-Oriented Programming (OOP) in Python

Introduction to OOP principles

Object-Oriented Programming (OOP) is a widely used programming paradigm that allows developers to model real-world entities as objects and encapsulate data and functionality within these objects. Python, a popular and versatile programming language, fully supports OOP principles, making it an excellent choice for developers interested in creating modular, maintainable, and scalable software. In this section, we will explore the fundamental OOP principles and how they are implemented in Python, providing insights into the advantages of using Python for OOP development.

One of the core concepts in OOP is the concept of "objects." In OOP, objects represent real-world entities or concepts and can be thought of as instances of classes. Classes act as blueprints or templates for creating objects and defining their attributes (data) and methods (functions). In Python, defining a class is straightforward; you use the class keyword followed by the class name, and within the class, you define its attributes and methods.

Encapsulation is a crucial OOP principle that emphasizes bundling data (attributes) and the methods that operate on that data into a single unit (the object). This bundling simplifies the code and ensures data integrity by controlling access to the data through methods. Python supports encapsulation by allowing you to define instance variables as attributes and methods within a class. By convention, instance variables are usually marked as private by prefixing them with an underscore, indicating that they should not be accessed directly from outside the class.

Inheritance is another essential OOP concept that enables the creation of new classes (subclass or derived class) that inherit attributes and methods from an existing class (base class or parent class). Python supports inheritance through a straightforward syntax, using the parent class's class name in the derived class's definition. Inheritance promotes code reusability and allows developers to effectively model hierarchical relationships between objects.

Polymorphism is a powerful OOP principle that treats objects of different classes as objects of a typical base class. In Python, polymorphism is achieved through method overriding and method overloading. Method overriding involves redefining a method in a derived class with the same name and parameters as the method in the base class. This enables the derived class to provide its own implementation while maintaining a consistent interface with the base class. Method overloading, on the other hand, is not directly supported in Python due to its dynamic typing system, but developers can achieve similar behavior by using default arguments or variable-length argument lists in methods.

Python's dynamic typing and duck typing contribute to its flexibility and support for polymorphism. Dynamic typing allows variables to change types during runtime, while duck typing focuses on the object's behavior rather than its type. This means that Python emphasizes the "if it looks like a duck, swims like a duck, and quacks like a duck, then it probably is a duck" philosophy. In other words, Python relies on an object's capabilities rather than its class hierarchy.

Abstraction simplifies complex systems by modeling them at a higher level of abstraction, hiding unnecessary details. In Python, abstraction is achieved by defining abstract base classes using the abc module. Abstract base classes provide a blueprint for other classes but cannot be instantiated themselves. Instead, they represent a set of methods that concrete subclasses must implement. This promotes code consistency and ensures that specific methods are available across different classes.

To demonstrate these OOP principles in Python, let's consider a simple example of a class hierarchy for representing different shapes. We can define a base class called Shape with attributes like color and methods like area and perimeter. Then, we can create subclasses such as Circle and Rectangle that inherit from Shape and provide their own implementations for the area and perimeter methods.

```python
from abc import ABC, abstractmethod


class Shape(ABC):

    def __init__(self, color):

        self.color = color


    @abstractmethod

    def area(self):

        pass
```

```python
    @abstractmethod
    def perimeter(self):
        pass

class Circle(Shape):
    def __init__(self, color, radius):
        super().__init__(color)
        self.radius = radius

    def area(self):
        return 3.14159265359 * self.radius ** 2

    def perimeter(self):
        return 2 * 3.14159265359 * self.radius

class Rectangle(Shape):
    def __init__(self, color, width, height):
        super().__init__(color)
        self.width = width
        self.height = height

    def area(self):
        return self.width * self.height
```

def perimeter(self):

return 2 * (self.width + self.height)

In this example, we have demonstrated encapsulation by encapsulating the attributes color, radius, width,
and height within their respective classes. Inheritance is evident in the fact that Circle and Rectangle inherit from the Shape class. Polymorphism is showcased as
both Circle and Rectangle have their own implementations of the area and perimeter methods, while abstraction is achieved by defining the abstract base class Shape with abstract methods.

In conclusion, Python provides a robust and flexible environment for implementing Object-Oriented Programming principles. Python empowers developers to create modular, maintainable, and extensible code by supporting encapsulation, inheritance, polymorphism, and abstraction. Understanding these OOP principles and their implementation in Python is essential for building effective software solutions and leveraging the full potential of this versatile programming language.

Creating classes and objects

In the realm of programming, especially in Object-Oriented Programming (OOP), the concept of creating classes and objects is fundamental. Classes and objects are the building blocks that allow developers to model real-world entities, encapsulate data and behavior, and structure their code for better organization and maintainability. In this section, we will delve into the intricacies of creating classes and objects, explore their significance in software development, and provide insights into how they are implemented in various programming languages, with a particular focus on Python.

At its core, a class can be thought of as a blueprint or template for creating objects. It defines the structure and behavior that its objects will possess. In essence, a class specifies the attributes (also known as properties or fields) that an object will have and the methods (functions) that an object can perform. Attributes represent the data associated with an object, while methods encapsulate the behavior or functionality. To illustrate this, consider a class representing a 'Car.' This class may have attributes like 'make,' 'model,' 'year,' and methods like 'start_engine' and 'drive.'

In Python, creating a class is straightforward. You use the class keyword followed by the class name, and within the class, you define its attributes and methods. Here's an example of a simple 'Car' class in Python:

```python
class Car:

    def __init__(self, make, model, year):

        self.make = make

        self.model = model

        self.year = year


    def start_engine(self):

        print(f"{self.make} {self.model}'s engine is now running.")

    def drive(self):

        print(f"{self.make} {self.model} is now in motion.")
```

In this example, we've defined a 'Car' class with attributes 'make,' 'model,' and 'year,' and two methods 'start_engine' and 'drive.' The __init__ method is a special method in Python known as a constructor, and it is called when an object of the class is created. It initializes the object's attributes with the values passed as arguments.

Once a class is defined, objects can be created from it. Objects are class instances and represent specific instances of the defined entity. To create an object, you simply call the class as if it were a function, passing any required arguments to the constructor. Here's how you can create a 'Car' object:

my_car = Car("Toyota", "Camry", 2022)

In this case, my_car is an instance of the 'Car' class, with its own attributes and methods. You can access the attributes using dot notation, and you can call the methods on the object:

print(my_car.make) # Output: Toyota

print(my_car.model) # Output: Camry

my_car.start_engine() # Output: Toyota Camry's engine is now running.

my_car.drive() # Output: Toyota Camry is now in motion.

Creating objects from a class is a fundamental concept in OOP, as it allows you to work with multiple instances of the same entity, each with its own unique data and behavior.

The importance of classes and objects in programming cannot be overstated. They provide a means of organizing and structuring code to mirror real-world entities and their interactions. This organization simplifies code maintenance, debugging, and collaboration among developers working on the same project. Moreover, classes and objects facilitate code reusability, as you can create new objects from existing classes, inheriting their attributes and methods, while also adding new functionality or customizing behavior as needed.

Inheritance is another critical concept closely related to classes and objects. It allows you to create new classes (known as derived or subclass) that inherit attributes and methods from an existing class (known as the base or parent class). This mechanism promotes code reuse and helps model hierarchical relationships between objects. In Python, you can specify the base class in the class definition, and the derived class will inherit all attributes and methods from the base class. You can then add additional attributes or methods to the derived class or override existing ones to provide specialized behavior.

For instance, in the context of our 'Car' class, you might want to create specialized subclasses like 'ElectricCar' and 'GasolineCar.' These subclasses can inherit attributes and methods from the 'Car' class but also include additional attributes like 'battery_capacity' for electric cars or 'fuel_type' for gasoline cars, along with methods specific to their respective types.

Here's an example of an 'ElectricCar' subclass:

```python
class ElectricCar(Car):

def __init__(self, make, model, year, battery_capacity):

super().__init__(make, model, year)

self.battery_capacity = battery_capacity


def charge(self):

print(f"{self.make} {self.model} is now charging.")
```

```python
# Creating an ElectricCar object

my_electric_car = ElectricCar("Tesla", "Model 3", 2023, 75)


# Accessing attributes and calling methods

print(my_electric_car.make) # Output: Tesla

print(my_electric_car.battery_capacity) # Output: 75

my_electric_car.charge() # Output: Tesla Model 3 is now charging.
```

In this example, the 'ElectricCar' class inherits from the 'Car' class, preserving its attributes and methods and introducing its own attributes and methods specific to electric cars.

In conclusion, creating classes and objects is a fundamental aspect of programming, especially in the context of Object-Oriented Programming. Classes define the structure and behavior of objects, while objects represent specific instances of those classes. They provide a structured and organized way to model real-world entities and their interactions in code. By incorporating concepts like inheritance, developers can create hierarchies of classes that promote code reusability and extensibility, making their code more efficient and maintainable. With its simple and elegant syntax, Python is an excellent language for implementing classes and objects, empowering developers to build modular and maintainable software systems. Understanding how to create and work with classes and objects is a crucial skill for any programmer, enabling them to design and implement effective software solutions.

Inheritance, polymorphism, and encapsulation

In Object-Oriented Programming (OOP), three fundamental concepts stand out as the cornerstones of software design and development: inheritance, polymorphism, and encapsulation. These principles are essential for creating modular, maintainable, and extensible code. In this section, we will explore each of these concepts in detail, discuss their significance in OOP, and provide insights into how they are implemented in various programming languages, focusing on their utilization in Python.

Inheritance is a concept that allows one class to inherit attributes and methods from another class. This mechanism enables code reuse and the modeling of hierarchical relationships between classes. Inheritance can be thought of as an "is-a" relationship, where a subclass is a specialized version of a superclass. Inheritance promotes the organization of code, as it allows developers to create new classes by building upon existing ones. In Python, inheritance is straightforward to implement using the class definition. A subclass is created by specifying the superclass in the class definition, and it automatically inherits all the attributes and methods of the superclass.

For example, consider a superclass called Vehicle that defines common attributes like 'make,' 'model,' and 'year.' We can create subclasses like Car and Motorcycle that inherit these attributes and can have their own additional attributes and methods. In Python, this would look like:

class Vehicle:

def __init__(self, make, model, year):

self.make = make

self.model = model

```python
 self.year = year

class Car(Vehicle):
def drive(self):
print(f"{self.make} {self.model} is now in motion.")


class Motorcycle(Vehicle):
def ride(self):
print(f"{self.make} {self.model} is now on the road.")
```

In this example, both the Car and Motorcycle classes inherit the make, model, and year attributes from the Vehicle superclass. This inheritance allows for code reuse and establishes a clear hierarchical relationship among these classes.

Polymorphism, another crucial OOP concept, refers to the ability of different classes to be treated as instances of a common base class. This allows for flexibility and code extensibility, as objects of various classes can be used interchangeably if they adhere to the same interface. Polymorphism is achieved through method overriding and method overloading. Method overriding involves redefining a method in a subclass with the same name and parameters as the method in the superclass. This enables the subclass to provide its own implementation while maintaining a consistent interface with the superclass.

Python's dynamic typing and duck typing contribute to its flexibility and support for polymorphism. Dynamic typing allows variables to change types during runtime, while duck typing focuses on an object's behavior rather than its type. In other words, if an object can perform a particular action, it is considered to have a specific behavior, regardless of its class hierarchy.

Encapsulation is the third cornerstone of OOP, emphasizing the bundling of data (attributes) and the methods that operate on that data into a single unit, known as an object. This bundling simplifies the code and ensures data integrity by controlling access to the data through methods. Python supports encapsulation by allowing the definition of instance variables as attributes and methods within a class. By convention, instance variables are often marked as private by prefixing them with an underscore, indicating that they should not be accessed directly from outside the class.

Let's explore an example that combines all three principles of inheritance, polymorphism, and encapsulation in Python:

```python
class Animal:

def __init__(self, name):

self.name = name


def speak(self):

pass


class Dog(Animal):

def speak(self):

return f"{self.name} says Woof!"


class Cat(Animal):
```

```python
    def speak(self):
        return f"{self.name} says Meow!"

# Usage of polymorphism
animals = [Dog("Buddy"), Cat("Whiskers")]

for animal in animals:
    print(animal.speak())

# Encapsulation example
class BankAccount:
    def __init__(self, account_holder, balance):
        self._account_holder = account_holder
        self._balance = balance

    def deposit(self, amount):
        if amount > 0:
            self._balance += amount

    def withdraw(self, amount):
        if amount > 0 and amount <= self._balance:
            self._balance -= amount

    def get_balance(self):
```

    return self._balance

```python
# Inheritance and encapsulation combined
class SavingsAccount(BankAccount):
    def __init__(self, account_holder, balance, interest_rate):
        super().__init__(account_holder, balance)
        self._interest_rate = interest_rate

    def apply_interest(self):
        self._balance += self._balance * (self._interest_rate / 100)


# Creating instances of SavingsAccount
savings_acc = SavingsAccount("Alice", 1000, 5)
savings_acc.apply_interest()
print(f"Account balance after interest: {savings_acc.get_balance()}")
```

In this example, we have an Animal superclass with subclasses Dog and Cat. The speak method is overridden in each subclass to provide specific behavior. We also have a BankAccount class demonstrating encapsulation, where access to the balance is controlled through methods. The SavingsAccount subclass inherits from BankAccount and adds an apply_interest method to calculate and apply interest.

In conclusion, inheritance, polymorphism, and encapsulation are fundamental concepts in Object-

Oriented Programming that enable developers to create modular, maintainable, and extensible code. Inheritance promotes code reuse and hierarchy modeling, polymorphism allows for flexible and interchangeable object usage, and encapsulation simplifies code while ensuring data integrity. With its dynamic typing and duck typing, Python provides a potent environment for implementing these principles effectively. Understanding and applying these concepts are essential skills for software developers, as they lead to well-organized, efficient, and maintainable codebases, facilitating the development of complex software systems.

CHAPTER VI

Exception Handling and Debugging

Handling errors and exceptions

Errors are an inevitable part of programming, and Python, like any other programming language, provides mechanisms for dealing with these errors. In Python, errors and exceptions are managed through a structured approach that allows developers to handle unexpected situations gracefully. This section will delve into the fundamental concepts of error handling and exception handling in Python, exploring how they work, why they are essential, and how they can be effectively employed.

Python is known for its simplicity and readability, and part of what makes it user-friendly is its built-in error handling system. When an error occurs during the execution of a Python program, it can disrupt the program's flow and potentially lead to unexpected crashes. To address this issue, Python offers a way to intercept and manage these errors known as exceptions.

Exceptions are objects in Python that represent errors or unexpected situations. When an exception occurs, it is said to be "raised." Python provides a mechanism for "catching" or "handling" these exceptions so the program can continue running without abruptly terminating. This process is accomplished using the try and except blocks.

The try block is where the code that may raise an exception is placed. It encloses the potentially problematic code, and if an exception is raised within this block, Python immediately transfers control to the except block, bypassing the remaining code within the try block. The except block contains the code that specifies how the program should respond to the raised exception.

For instance, consider a scenario where a program attempts to open a file that does not exist. Without proper error handling, this situation could lead to a crash. However, using exceptions, we can gracefully handle this error:

try:

file = open("non_existent_file.txt", "r")

except FileNotFoundError:

print("File not found.")

In this example, the try block attempts to open the file "non_existent_file.txt" for reading. If the file does not exist, a FileNotFoundError exception is raised, and the program jumps to the except block, which prints an informative error message.

Python provides a wide range of built-in exceptions to cover various types of errors. These exceptions are organized in a hierarchy, with the base class being BaseException. Derived from BaseException are multiple subclasses, such as Exception, TypeError, ValueError, and many more, each catering to specific error scenarios. Developers can also create custom exceptions by defining new classes that inherit from Exception or one of its subclasses.

In addition to the except block, Python allows the use of else and finally blocks in exception handling. The else block is executed if no exceptions are raised within the try block. It is useful for specifying code that should run only when no exceptions occur. The finally block is always executed, regardless of whether an exception is raised or not. It is often employed to perform cleanup operations, such as closing files or releasing resources.

Here is an example that demonstrates the use of else and finally blocks:

```python
try:

result = 10 / 2

except ZeroDivisionError:

print("Cannot divide by zero.")

else:

print(f"Result: {result}")

finally:

print("Execution completed.")
```

In this example, the try block divides 10 by 2, which does not raise any exceptions. Therefore, the else block is executed, displaying the result. Afterward, the finally block is executed to signify the completion of execution, regardless of the outcome.

Another important aspect of Python's exception handling is the concept of exception propagation. When an exception is raised but not caught within a function, it is propagated up the call stack to the calling functions. This allows for higher-level code to handle exceptions if needed. If an exception is not caught at all, the program will terminate, and Python will display an error message.

To illustrate exception propagation, consider the following example:

```python
def divide(a, b):

return a / b
```

```python
try:

result = divide(10, 0)

except ZeroDivisionError:

print("Cannot divide by zero.")

else:

print(f"Result: {result}")
```

In this case, the divide function attempts to divide 10 by 0, resulting in a ZeroDivisionError exception. Since this exception is not caught within the function, it is propagated up to the try block in the calling code, where it is caught and the appropriate error message is printed.

In addition to handling exceptions using try, except, else, and finally, Python provides a way to raise exceptions using the raise statement explicitly. This allows developers to create custom exceptions or re-raise exceptions after handling them.

For instance, here's how a custom exception can be raised:

```python
class CustomError(Exception):

pass


def example_function():

raise CustomError("This is a custom exception.")


try:

example_function()
```

except CustomError as e:

print(f"Custom Error: {e}")

In this example, the CustomError class is defined by inheriting from the base Exception class, and the example_function raises an instance of this custom exception. When the exception is caught in the except block, it allows for specific handling and can provide custom error messages or additional information.

In conclusion, handling errors and exceptions is fundamental to writing robust and reliable Python programs. Python's built-in exception handling mechanism, including try, except, else, and finally blocks, allows developers to manage errors and recover from unexpected situations gracefully. By understanding how exceptions work and employing best practices in error handling, programmers can create more resilient and user-friendly Python applications. Whether it's dealing with built-in exceptions or creating custom ones, mastering error handling is essential for writing high-quality Python code that stands up to real-world challenges.

Debugging techniques and tools

Debugging is an essential skill for every programmer, and Python, as a versatile and widely used programming language, offers a variety of techniques and tools to help developers identify and resolve errors in their code. Effective debugging saves time and contributes to the creation of more reliable and robust Python applications. This section will explore debugging techniques and tools in Python, covering both the built-in debugging capabilities of the language and external debugging tools that can enhance the debugging process.

One of Python's most fundamental debugging techniques is using print statements. Print statements allow developers to inspect variables' values and their code's flow. By strategically placing print statements at different points in the code, developers can track the program's execution and identify any unexpected behavior or errors. This method is simple yet effective, especially for beginners, and it provides insights into the program's state during execution.

For example, consider the following code snippet:

def divide(a, b):

result = a / b

print(f"Result: {result}")

return result

numerator = 10

denominator = 2

result = divide(numerator, denominator)

In this code, a print statement is used to display the result of the division operation, allowing the developer to verify the intermediate values and identify any issues that may arise during execution.

While print statements are useful, they have limitations, such as not being able to inspect complex data structures or track the flow of the program in detail. To address these limitations, Python provides a built-in debugging module called pdb (Python Debugger). The pdb module allows developers to set breakpoints in their code, step through code execution, inspect variables, and even change variable values during debugging.

Here's an example of using the pdb module to debug a simple function:

```python
import pdb


def divide(a, b):

result = a / b

pdb.set_trace() # Set a breakpoint

return result


numerator = 10

denominator = 0

result = divide(numerator, denominator)
```

In this code, the pdb.set_trace() line sets a breakpoint, causing the program to pause execution and enter an interactive debugging session when it reaches that point. Within the debugging session, developers can use various commands to inspect variables, step through code, and identify the source of errors.

In addition to the built-in pdb module, Python also offers a popular third-party debugger called pdb++. pdb++ extends the functionality of pdb by providing a more user-friendly and feature-rich debugging experience. It offers tab-completion, better variable visualization, and improved command syntax, making debugging in Python more efficient and effective.

Beyond the built-in and third-party debugging modules, Python developers can also utilize Integrated Development Environments (IDEs) and code editors that offer built-in debugging support. IDEs like PyCharm, Visual Studio Code, and PyDev provide powerful debugging features, including visual breakpoints, variable inspection, and call stack exploration. These tools streamline the debugging process and enhance productivity, making them popular choices for Python development.

Another valuable tool in the Python debugging toolbox is the use of assertions. Assertions are statements that check whether a given condition is true, and if not, they raise an exception. While assertions are typically used for testing and validation, they can also be employed for debugging purposes to identify unexpected program states or conditions that should not occur.

Here's an example of using assertions for debugging:

```python
def calculate_average(numbers):

assert len(numbers) > 0, "List of numbers must not be empty"
total = sum(numbers)

return total / len(numbers)


data = [10, 20, 30, 40, 50]

average = calculate_average(data)
```

In this code, an assertion is used to check if the list of numbers is empty before calculating the average. If the assertion fails, it raises an AssertionError with a custom error message, helping developers pinpoint the issue.

In addition to these debugging techniques, Python developers can use external debugging tools like pdb++, pyflame, and py-spy for performance profiling. These tools allow developers to analyze the runtime behavior of their Python applications, identify performance bottlenecks, and optimize their code for better performance.

In conclusion, debugging is an essential part of software development, and Python offers a range of techniques and tools to help developers identify and resolve errors effectively. From simple print statements to the powerful pdb module and feature-rich IDEs, Python developers have various options for debugging their code. By mastering these debugging techniques and tools, developers can streamline their workflow, save time, and create more reliable Python applications. Debugging is not just a skill; it's a crucial aspect of writing high-quality and maintainable code in Python.

Writing robust and error-resistant code

Writing Python code that is robust and resistant to errors is a fundamental skill for developers. Robust code functions correctly and gracefully handles unexpected situations and edge cases, ensuring the stability and reliability of applications. This section will explore the principles and techniques for writing robust and error-resistant code in Python.

One of the key principles in writing robust code is to validate and sanitize inputs. When developing Python applications, it is essential to assume that external inputs, whether from users, files, or network sources, may be unreliable or malicious. To mitigate potential issues, developers should validate and sanitize input data thoroughly. This includes checking for data types, bounds, and potential security vulnerabilities like SQL injection or cross-site scripting (XSS). By validating inputs, developers can prevent many common errors and security vulnerabilities.

For instance, if a Python web application accepts user input through a form, validating and sanitizing the data before processing it can prevent SQL injection attacks. Using libraries like SQLAlchemy or Django's Object-Relational Mapping (ORM) can help sanitize database queries and protect against potential security threats.

Error handling and exception management are other crucial aspects of writing robust Python code. As discussed in a previous section, exception handling is vital for gracefully handling unexpected errors and ensuring that the application does not crash abruptly. Robust code should be prepared to handle exceptions that may occur during execution and provide informative error messages or fallback mechanisms to maintain functionality. Consider the following example of robust code that handles potential exceptions when reading a file:

```python
try:

with open("data.txt", "r") as file:

content = file.read()

except FileNotFoundError:

print("The file 'data.txt' does not exist.")

except IOError as e:

print(f"An error occurred while reading the file: {e}")

else:

# Process the file content

process_data(content)
```

In this code, exceptions like FileNotFoundError and IOError are caught and handled, ensuring the program responds appropriately to various error scenarios. The else block contains the code for processing the file content, which is executed only if no exceptions occur.

Furthermore, robust code should implement proper error logging. Logging is a valuable practice that helps developers diagnose issues in production environments. Python's built-in logging module provides a powerful way to log information, warnings, errors, and other messages from the application. By logging errors and exceptions, developers can gather valuable insights into what went wrong, when it happened, and how often specific issues occur.

Here's an example of setting up error logging in Python:

```python
import logging


# Configure the logging settings

logging.basicConfig(filename='error_log.txt',
level=logging.ERROR)


def divide(a, b):

try:

result = a / b

except ZeroDivisionError:

logging.error("Division by zero error")

result = None

return result
```

In this code, the logging module configures error logging to a file named "error_log.txt" at the ERROR level. When a ZeroDivisionError occurs during the divide function's execution, an error message is logged, providing valuable information for debugging and troubleshooting.

Another essential practice for writing robust Python code is to perform automated testing. Automated testing, including unit, integration, and regression tests, helps ensure that code behaves as expected and that changes or updates do not introduce new errors. Python's unittest and pytest libraries are commonly used for writing and executing tests, allowing developers to create a suite of tests to validate different parts of their codebase.

Additionally, Python's docstring conventions, such as using docstrings to describe functions and methods, are essential for code documentation and understanding. Proper documentation helps other developers understand the purpose and usage of functions and enables tools like Sphinx to generate comprehensive documentation for libraries and applications.

Furthermore, adhering to coding standards and best practices is critical for writing robust code. Python has a well-defined style guide called PEP 8 (Python Enhancement Proposal 8), which provides recommendations on code formatting, naming conventions, and other aspects of coding style. Following PEP 8 guidelines and adopting consistent coding practices across the codebase helps make the code more readable, maintainable, and less prone to errors.

Additionally, Python's type hints, introduced in PEP 484, can improve code robustness by specifying the expected types of function arguments and return values. While type hints are not enforced at runtime, tools like mypy can be used to perform static type checking and catch type-related errors before running the code.

In summary, writing robust and error-resistant code in Python is a multifaceted process involving input validation, error handling, logging, automated testing, documentation, adherence to coding standards, and type hints. Collectively, these practices contribute to creating

Python applications that are reliable, maintainable, and less prone to errors. By following these principles and techniques, developers can develop high-quality Python code that works correctly and stands up to real-world challenges and changes over time. Ultimately, writing robust code is an investment in the long-term success and stability of Python projects.

CHAPTER VII

List Comprehensions and Generators

List comprehensions for concise code

List comprehensions are a powerful and concise feature in Python that allows developers to create lists more efficiently and readably. Python is known for its simplicity and readability; list comprehensions are a perfect example of this philosophy in action. With list comprehensions, you can perform complex operations on lists with just a single line of code, making your programs more concise and easier to understand.

One of the main benefits of using list comprehensions is their ability to replace traditional for loops when creating lists. In a conventional for loop, you would need to write multiple lines of code to iterate through a list, perform some operation on each element, and then append the result to a new list. This can quickly become cumbersome and difficult to read, especially for more complex operations. On the other hand, list comprehensions allow you to achieve the same result in a single line of code, making your code more concise and easier to maintain.

The syntax for a list comprehension in Python is quite simple. It consists of square brackets enclosing an expression, followed by a for clause, and optionally, one or more for or if clauses. The expression inside the square brackets is evaluated for each item in the iterable specified in the for clause, and the results are collected into a new list. For example, you can use a list comprehension to create a list of squares for a given range of numbers like this:

squares = [x ** 2 for x in range(1, 11)]

In this example, the list comprehension generates a list of squares for the numbers 1 through 10. It's a concise and elegant way to perform this operation, and it's easy to understand at a glance.

List comprehensions are not limited to simple arithmetic operations; they can also be used to filter and transform data. For instance, you can use list comprehension to filter out all the even numbers from a list and create a new list containing only the odd numbers:

numbers = [1, 2, 3, 4, 5, 6, 7, 8, 9, 10]

odd_numbers = [x for x in numbers if x % 2 != 0]

In this example, the list comprehension filters out the even numbers from the original list, leaving us with a list of odd numbers. This can be extremely useful when processing data and extracting specific elements that meet certain criteria.

List comprehensions also work with more complex data structures like nested lists. You can use nested list comprehensions to flatten a list of lists or perform operations on nested elements. For instance, if you have a list of lists and you want to flatten it into a single list, you can use a nested list comprehension like this:
nested_lists = [[1, 2, 3], [4, 5, 6], [7, 8, 9]]

flat_list = [x for sublist in nested_lists for x in sublist]

In this example, the nested list comprehension iterates through each sublist in the nested_lists and then iterates through the elements within each sublist, effectively flattening the list into a single one.

Another advantage of list comprehensions is their performance. List comprehensions are often faster and more efficient than equivalent for loops. Python's internal optimizations make list comprehensions a preferred choice for creating lists, especially when dealing with large datasets.

List comprehensions can also make your code more readable by reducing the number of lines and improving the overall structure. Instead of scattering for loops and append statements throughout your code, you can use list comprehensions to consolidate the list creation process into a single, easily understandable line of code.

However, it's worth noting that while list comprehensions are a powerful tool, they are not always the best choice for every situation. Sometimes, using a traditional for loop may be more appropriate, especially when the logic becomes too complex to fit into a single line or when you must perform multiple operations on each item.

In conclusion, list comprehensions are a concise and elegant feature in Python that allows you to create lists with ease and readability. They often replace traditional for loops, making your code more concise, efficient, and easier to understand. Whether you need to perform simple arithmetic operations, filter and transform data, or work with nested lists, list comprehensions can simplify your code and improve its performance. By mastering this feature, you can become a more efficient Python programmer and write powerful and expressive code.

Generators for memory-efficient processing

Generators are a fundamental Python feature that enables memory-efficient processing of large datasets and iterative operations. Python is widely recognized for its simplicity and readability, and generators exemplify this principle by providing a clean and efficient solution for tasks that involve large amounts of data. With generators, you can generate data on-the-fly, avoiding the need to store it all in memory, which is particularly beneficial when dealing with extensive or continuously streaming data sources.

One of the primary advantages of generators is their ability to produce values lazily, as they are needed. In contrast to lists or other data structures, which store all elements in memory simultaneously, generators yield values one at a time when requested. This means that you can process data without worrying about running out of memory, even when working with enormous datasets. Generators are especially valuable when handling files, databases, or data streams, as they allow you to iterate through data without loading it entirely into memory.

The syntax for defining a generator in Python is quite similar to that of a regular function, using the yield keyword. The yield statement allows a function to "pause" and save its state, enabling it to resume execution from where it left off when called again. This mechanism is the core of generators and what makes them memory-efficient. Here's a simple example of a generator that yields the squares of numbers from 1 to N:

```python
def generate_squares(N):

for i in range(1, N + 1):

yield i ** 2
```

When you call this generator function, it does not immediately calculate and store all the squares in memory. Instead, it yields each square one by one as you iterate through it, making it efficient even for large values of N.

Generators are not only about memory efficiency; they also contribute to code clarity and maintainability. You can separate concerns and create more modular code by encapsulating the logic for generating data within a generator. This separation of concerns makes it easier to reason about your code, test individual components, and reuse generator functions across different parts of your program.

In addition to simple generators, Python also provides generator expressions, which are concise and convenient for creating generators inline. A generator expression is similar to a list comprehension but with parentheses instead of square brackets. For instance, you can create a generator that yields the squares of numbers from 1 to N using a generator expression like this:

```python
squares_generator = (i ** 2 for i in range(1, N + 1))
```

This concise syntax is particularly useful when you need a generator for a one-time use or when creating a generator on the fly.

Another advantage of generators is their ability to implement infinite sequences. Since generators generate values lazily, you can create generators that produce an infinite data stream without consuming infinite memory. For example, you can define a generator that yields an infinite sequence of Fibonacci numbers:

```python
def fibonacci():

a, b = 0, 1

while True:

yield a

a, b = b, a + b
```

In this example, the fibonacci generator produces Fibonacci numbers indefinitely, and you can use it in your code without worrying about memory limitations.

While generators are a powerful tool for memory-efficient processing, they also come with some trade-offs. Since they are stateful and maintain their context, you can iterate through a generator only once. You must recreate the generator if you need to reuse the same data. Generators are generally slower than processing data stored in memory, as they involve function calls and state management. Therefore, they are most suitable for scenarios where memory efficiency is a primary concern.

In conclusion, generators in Python are a vital feature for memory-efficient processing, enabling the handling of large datasets and infinite sequences without overwhelming system memory. They contribute to clean and modular code by encapsulating data generation logic and allowing for on-the-fly generation. Whether you're working with files, databases, or continuous data streams, generators are a valuable tool that can improve the efficiency and maintainability of your Python code. By mastering the use of generators, you can become a more effective Python programmer, capable of handling resource-intensive tasks with elegance and simplicity.

Use cases and examples

List comprehensions and generators are powerful and versatile features in Python that streamline and enhance how we manipulate and generate data. Each has its unique strengths and use cases, making them essential tools in a Python programmer's toolkit. In this section, we will explore the use cases and examples of list comprehensions and generators, highlighting their benefits and illustrating when to employ each one.

List comprehensions are particularly useful when you need to create a new list by applying an operation to each element of an existing iterable. They offer a concise and readable way to achieve this, often replacing the need for traditional for loops. For example, consider a scenario where you have a list of numbers and want to create a new list containing the squares of these numbers. Using a list comprehension, you can accomplish this task elegantly:

numbers = [1, 2, 3, 4, 5]

squares = [x ** 2 for x in numbers]

List comprehensions are not limited to basic arithmetic operations; they can also handle more complex transformations and filtering. For instance, you can use a list comprehension to filter out even numbers from a list:
numbers = [1, 2, 3, 4, 5, 6, 7, 8, 9]

odd_numbers = [x for x in numbers if x % 2 != 0]

In this case, the list comprehension efficiently creates a new list containing only the odd numbers from the original list.

Another strength of list comprehensions is their ability to work with nested data structures. Suppose you have a list of lists and want to flatten it into a single list. A nested list comprehension allows you to achieve this:
nested_lists = [[1, 2], [3, 4], [5, 6]]

flat_list = [x for sublist in nested_lists for x in sublist]

This concise syntax simplifies complex operations, making your code more readable and maintainable.
On the other hand, generators are ideal when memory efficiency is a concern or when working with large datasets or infinite sequences. Generators produce values on-the-fly, rather than storing them all in memory simultaneously. This memory-saving characteristic makes them invaluable in situations where memory resources are limited. For instance, if you need to process a large file line by line, you can use a generator to read and yield each line as needed, ensuring efficient memory usage: def

read_lines(filename):

```python
 with open(filename, 'r') as file:

for line in file:

yield line
```

Generators are also perfect for creating infinite sequences. For example, you can define a generator that produces an infinite sequence of Fibonacci numbers:

```python
def fibonacci():

a, b = 0, 1

while True:

yield a

a, b = b, a + b
```

In this case, the fibonacci generator can generate Fibonacci numbers indefinitely without consuming excessive memory.

Moreover, generators are beneficial for simplifying the handling of data streams, such as data retrieved from APIs or continuously updated sources. You can use generators to process and yield data as it arrives, ensuring your program remains responsive and memory-efficient.

While list comprehensions and generators each have their strengths and use cases, choosing the right tool for the job is essential. List comprehensions excel at transforming and filtering data from existing iterables, providing a concise and readable syntax. They are suitable for tasks that don't involve large datasets or extensive memory usage.

On the other hand, generators shine in scenarios where memory efficiency is crucial, or when dealing with vast amounts of data, streaming data sources, or infinite sequences. Their ability to generate data lazily and on-the-fly ensures efficient resource utilization.

In summary, list comprehensions and generators are essential features in Python, offering potent solutions to different programming challenges. List comprehensions simplify the creation of new lists by applying operations to existing data, while generators provide memory-efficient processing for large datasets and infinite sequences. By understanding their strengths and use cases, Python developers can make informed decisions on when and how to employ these versatile tools, ultimately enhancing code readability, maintainability, and performance.

CHAPTER VIII

Performance Optimization

Profiling and benchmarking Python code

Python, a high-level, interpreted programming language, has gained immense popularity among developers for its simplicity, readability, and versatility. However, as applications grow in complexity and data volumes increase, the need for efficient and optimized code becomes paramount. Profiling and benchmarking are two essential techniques that empower developers to identify bottlenecks, maximize performance, and ensure Python code runs as efficiently as possible.

Profiling is the process of analyzing code execution to identify performance bottlenecks and areas for improvement. Python offers several profiling tools that help developers pinpoint where their code spends the most time and resources. One such tool is cProfile, a built-in module that provides a detailed breakdown of function calls, execution time, and the number of times each function is called. By running cProfile on your code, you can identify which functions or sections of code consume the most CPU time, enabling you to focus your optimization efforts effectively.

Another popular profiling tool for Python is Pyflame, which can provide flame graphs, a visualization technique that helps developers identify performance bottlenecks more intuitively. Flame graphs display the call stack of your code, making it easier to see which functions are called most frequently and where the program spends the most time. Profiling tools like Pyflame allow developers to identify bottlenecks and prioritize which parts of the codebase need optimization for maximum performance gains.

Once bottlenecks have been identified through profiling, the next step is benchmarking. Benchmarking involves comparing different implementations or code snippets to determine which performs better in execution time or resource usage. Python offers various benchmarking tools, such as the timeit module, which allows developers to measure the execution time of specific code segments accurately. By comparing the performance of different implementations or optimization strategies, developers can decide which approach to pursue.

Additionally, libraries like pytest-benchmark provide a convenient way to automate benchmarking tests and collect performance data over time. This enables developers to track the impact of code changes on performance continuously and helps prevent performance regressions. Effective benchmarking ensures that code optimizations are effective and provides a baseline for future improvements.

Profiling and benchmarking go hand in hand when it comes to optimizing Python code. Profiling helps identify performance bottlenecks, while benchmarking allows developers to evaluate the effectiveness of different optimization strategies. These techniques are particularly crucial in Python, where the language's dynamic nature and the Global Interpreter Lock (GIL) can introduce performance challenges.

The Global Interpreter Lock (GIL) is a critical factor in Python's performance that developers must consider. It ensures that only one thread can execute Python bytecode at a time, which can limit the effectiveness of multi-threading for CPU-bound tasks. Profiling can help uncover instances where the GIL is a limiting factor in your code's performance, allowing you to explore alternative concurrency models, such as multiprocessing or asynchronous programming, to improve performance.

In addition to optimizing CPU-bound tasks, profiling and benchmarking are invaluable for optimizing memory usage. Python's memory management, based on reference counting and garbage collection, can lead to memory leaks and inefficient memory usage if improperly handled. Profiling tools like memory_profiler can help identify memory-intensive parts of your code, enabling you to take corrective measures, such as optimizing data structures or releasing unnecessary references, to reduce memory consumption.

Furthermore, profiling and benchmarking can be essential when working with external libraries or frameworks in Python. Many Python applications rely on third-party packages, and understanding how these libraries impact performance is crucial. Profiling tools can reveal how much time your code spends within library functions, helping you make informed decisions about optimizing your code or exploring alternative libraries for better performance.

Optimizing Python code through profiling and benchmarking is an iterative process. After making optimizations based on profiling results, developers should re-run benchmarks to ensure that performance improvements have been achieved. Continuous profiling and benchmarking should also be integrated into the development workflow to prevent performance regressions as the codebase evolves.

In conclusion, profiling and benchmarking are essential techniques for optimizing Python code. Profiling tools like cProfile and Pyflame help identify performance bottlenecks, while benchmarking allows developers to compare different optimization strategies and track performance improvements. These techniques are particularly valuable in Python due to the language's unique characteristics, such as the Global Interpreter Lock and dynamic typing. By incorporating profiling and benchmarking into their development process, Python developers can ensure that their code runs efficiently and meets performance requirements, even as applications grow in complexity and data volumes increase.

Strategies for optimizing code execution

Python, known for its simplicity and readability, has become one of the most popular programming languages in the world. However, its interpreted nature and dynamic typing can lead to performance challenges, especially when dealing with large datasets or computationally intensive tasks. To ensure that Python code runs efficiently, developers often need to employ various strategies for code optimization.

One of the fundamental strategies for optimizing Python code execution is using appropriate data structures and algorithms. Choosing the right data structure for a specific task can significantly impact performance. For example, a dictionary for quick key-value lookups or a set for membership tests is more efficient than a list. Similarly, selecting the appropriate algorithm for a given problem, such as sorting or searching, can lead to substantial performance improvements.

In addition to data structures and algorithms, developers should be mindful of Python's built-in functions and libraries. Python's Standard Library offers a wide range of functions that are optimized for various operations. Utilizing these built-in functions instead of reinventing the wheel with custom implementations can often lead to faster code execution. For instance, the sum() function is optimized for calculating the sum of an iterable, and the join() method is the most efficient way to concatenate strings.

Furthermore, leveraging external libraries can significantly enhance code performance. Python has a vast ecosystem of third-party libraries, such as NumPy for numerical computations and Pandas for data manipulation. These libraries are implemented in lower- level languages like C and C++, making them highly efficient for their respective domains. Integrating these libraries into your codebase can substantially improve speed without sacrificing Python's high-level expressiveness.

Another crucial strategy for code optimization is to minimize unnecessary work. Python developers often emphasize the importance of "lazy evaluation." This means that computations should only be performed when their results are actually needed. For example, when working with large datasets, you can use generators or iterators to load and process data in smaller, manageable chunks, rather than loading the entire dataset into memory at once. You can significantly improve code efficiency by avoiding unnecessary memory consumption and computations.

Caching is another powerful technique for reducing redundant work. Python provides caching mechanisms like memoization, which stores the results of expensive function calls and returns cached results when the same inputs are reencountered. Caching can be particularly beneficial in recursive algorithms or functions with expensive calculations, as it eliminates the need to recompute results for previously seen inputs.

Furthermore, developers should know the importance of profiling and benchmarking, as discussed in the previous section. Profiling helps identify performance bottlenecks, allowing developers to focus their optimization efforts on the most critical parts of the code. Conversely, benchmarking allows for objective comparisons of different optimization strategies to ensure that improvements are achieved.

For CPU-bound tasks, parallelization and concurrency can be valuable strategies for optimization. Python's Global Interpreter Lock (GIL) limits the execution of Python bytecode to a single thread at a time, hindering multi-threading for CPU-bound tasks. However, Python offers alternatives such as multiprocessing and asynchronous programming using libraries like asyncio. These approaches enable parallel execution, using multi-core processors better and improving code performance.

Moreover, optimizing memory usage is crucial, especially when dealing with large datasets or long-running processes. Python's memory management relies on reference counting and garbage collection, which can lead to memory leaks if not managed carefully. Developers should be vigilant in releasing unnecessary references, using context managers and the with statement to ensure timely resource cleanup, and employing tools like memory_profiler to identify and rectify memory-intensive code sections.

Lastly, code optimization should not come at the expense of code readability and maintainability. While optimizing for performance is essential, it should not lead to overly complex or convoluted code. Developers must balance performance and maintainability to ensure that code remains understandable and adaptable over time.

In conclusion, optimizing code execution in Python requires a multifaceted approach. Choosing the right data structures, algorithms, built-in functions, and utilizing external libraries can provide significant performance gains. Minimizing unnecessary work through lazy evaluation, caching, and proper memory management is essential for efficient code execution. Profiling, benchmarking, parallelization, and concurrency are valuable tools for identifying and addressing performance bottlenecks. Ultimately, the key to successful code optimization in Python is finding the right balance between performance improvements and code maintainability, ensuring that applications run smoothly and efficiently while remaining readable and adaptable.

Using libraries and modules for performance gains

Python's versatility and extensive standard library make it popular for various applications, from web development to data analysis and scientific computing. However, when dealing with computationally intensive tasks or large-scale data processing, Python's interpreted nature can sometimes lead to suboptimal performance. To address this challenge, developers can harness the power of external libraries and modules, which are pre-written, optimized pieces of code designed to perform specific tasks efficiently. This section explores the significance of using libraries and modules for performance gains in Python and provides insights into some of the most commonly employed ones.

One of the primary advantages of using external libraries and modules is that they are often implemented in lower-level languages like C or C++, which execute significantly faster than Python's interpreted bytecode. These libraries take advantage of the performance optimizations these lower-level languages provide, resulting in faster execution times for specific tasks. A prime example of this is NumPy, a library for numerical computations in Python.

NumPy provides high-performance, multidimensional arrays and a wide range of mathematical functions, making it an indispensable tool for data scientists, engineers, and researchers. By utilizing NumPy, developers can perform array operations much more efficiently than using Python's built-in lists, as NumPy's underlying C implementation optimizes memory management and computational efficiency.

Another critical aspect of external libraries and modules is their specialization in specific domains. These libraries are often developed and maintained by experts in their respective fields, ensuring they are both feature-rich and performance-oriented. For instance, Pandas is a go-to library when working with data manipulation and analysis. Pandas offers data structures like DataFrames that allow for efficient data indexing, selection, and aggregation. Behind the scenes, Pandas leverages NumPy for numerical operations, further enhancing its computational speed. Thanks to its specialized design for data-related tasks, developers can confidently rely on Pandas to handle large datasets efficiently.

Furthermore, libraries and modules contribute to code reusability and maintainability. By incorporating well-established libraries into your codebase, you benefit from their performance optimizations and reduce the need to reinvent the wheel. This approach saves development time and effort and minimizes the chances of introducing errors. For instance, when developing web applications in Python, the Flask or Django frameworks provide a wealth of functionality for handling routing, authentication, and database interactions. These frameworks have been extensively tested and optimized for web development, allowing developers to focus on application-specific logic rather than low-level infrastructure.

In addition to domain-specific libraries, Python offers many general-purpose libraries that can be immensely valuable for various tasks. The standard library includes modules like collections, itertools, and datetime that provide efficient tools for data manipulation, iteration, and time handling. External libraries such as Requests for HTTP requests, Matplotlib for data visualization, and Scikit-learn for machine learning further expand Python's capabilities and performance potential. These libraries have gained widespread adoption due to their robustness and efficiency.

Moreover, the Python Package Index (PyPI) is a treasure trove of third-party libraries contributed by the Python community. Developers can easily access and incorporate these libraries into their projects using package managers like pip. This vibrant ecosystem ensures that developers have access to a wide array of tools and libraries tailored to their specific needs, from natural language processing with NLTK to deep learning with TensorFlow or PyTorch.

Another advantage of using external libraries is the opportunity for parallelization and concurrency. Python's Global Interpreter Lock (GIL) can limit multi-threading for CPU-bound tasks, but some libraries and modules are designed to circumvent this limitation. The multiprocessing module allows developers to create multiple processes that run concurrently, using all available CPU cores. Libraries like Dask and joblib also provide parallel computing capabilities for tasks involving parallelizable computations or data processing pipelines. These libraries enable Python developers to harness the power of parallelization without being hindered by the GIL.

Furthermore, external libraries often come with robust documentation and active communities, which are invaluable resources for developers seeking guidance and support. Documentation provides clear instructions on using the library's features and functions effectively, while community forums and mailing lists offer a platform for developers to seek help, share knowledge, and collaborate with others. This accessibility ensures that developers can leverage libraries to their full potential and troubleshoot any issues they encounter along the way.

In conclusion, utilizing external libraries and modules is a cornerstone of optimizing code performance in Python. These pre-written, specialized pieces of code offer efficient solutions for specific tasks and are often implemented in lower-level languages to maximize computational speed. Whether it's numerical computations with NumPy, data manipulation with Pandas, web development with Flask or Django, or machine learning with Scikit-learn, Python's rich ecosystem of libraries empowers developers to build high-performance applications without sacrificing readability or maintainability. Additionally, libraries provide opportunities for parallelization and concurrency, helping Python developers make the most of multi-core processors. By embracing these libraries and modules, Python developers can leverage the collective knowledge and expertise of the Python community to create efficient, robust, and feature-rich software solutions.

CHAPTER IX

Pythonic Patterns and Best Practices

Pythonic coding style and conventions

Python, renowned for its readability and elegance, emphasizes the importance of a coding style that is both consistent and adheres to specific conventions. The term "Pythonic" refers to code that works and follows the idiomatic and stylistic guidelines set forth by the Python community. Adopting a Pythonic coding style improves the readability and maintainability of code and fosters a sense of unity within the Python ecosystem. In this section, we will explore the principles of Pythonic coding style and conventions, examining their significance and providing insights into some of the key guidelines.

One of the foundational principles of Pythonic coding is the use of meaningful and descriptive variable and function names. Python encourages developers to use clear and concise names that convey the purpose and content of variables, functions, and classes. By doing so, code becomes self-documenting, making it easier for others (and your future self) to understand the code without extensive comments or documentation. For instance, instead of using cryptic variable names like "x" or "temp," Pythonic code would use names like "user_input" or "result" to enhance clarity and readability.

Another essential aspect of Pythonic coding is adhering to the PEP 8 style guide, which outlines code layout, naming conventions, and code organization conventions. PEP 8 is a reference for Python developers worldwide and promotes a consistent coding style across projects. By following PEP 8 guidelines, Pythonic code exhibits uniformity in indentation (using spaces instead of tabs), adheres to a maximum line length of 79 characters (or 72 for docstrings), and employs consistent naming conventions (e.g., lowercase_with_underscores for variable and function names, CamelCase for class names).

Pythonic code also embraces the use of list comprehensions and generator expressions to streamline operations on sequences. These concise and expressive constructs make the code more readable and often result in improved performance. Instead of using verbose loops to filter or transform data, Python developers use list comprehensions to achieve the same results with fewer lines of code. For example, a list comprehension can be used to create a new list of squared numbers from an existing list in a single line of code.

In addition to list comprehensions, Pythonic code leverages the power of the built-in functions and modules available in the Python Standard Library. These functions, such as map(), filter(), and reduce(), enable developers to perform common operations efficiently and succinctly. For instance, the any() and all() functions allow for easy testing of conditions in iterable objects, while the enumerate() function simplifies iteration over both the index and value of elements in a sequence.

Pythonic coding style promotes the use of exception handling for error control, rather than relying on conditional statements to preemptively check for potential errors. This approach follows the "Easier to Ask for Forgiveness than Permission" (EAFP) principle. By attempting an operation and catching exceptions when they occur, Pythonic code remains concise and avoids the need for extensive if-else checks. Using specific exception types and well-crafted error messages further enhances code quality and debugging.

Moreover, Pythonic code prioritizes using context managers, enabled by the with statement. Context managers, implemented through the __enter__() and __exit__() methods, simplify resource management, such as file handling or database connections. By using context managers, developers ensure that resources are properly acquired and released, promoting clean and error-free code.

One of the most celebrated features of Pythonic code is the emphasis on readability through the use of whitespace and indentation. Python enforces strict indentation rules, requiring consistent and meaningful whitespace to structure code blocks. This practice contributes to the visual clarity of the code and eliminates the need for explicit block delimiters like braces or keywords. The use of meaningful indentation is a hallmark of Python's design philosophy, making code visually intuitive and reducing the likelihood of syntax errors.

Additionally, Pythonic code encourages using docstrings, which are string literals that document functions, classes, and modules. Docstrings are accessible through the built-in help() function and serve as self-contained documentation for code elements. Pythonic developers make it easier for others to understand and use their code effectively by documenting code with clear and informative docstrings.

Furthermore, Pythonic code embraces the concept of "flat is better than nested." This principle encourages developers to minimize levels of nesting and indentation within their code. By avoiding excessive nesting, code becomes more readable and maintains a shallower and more linear structure. Deeply nested code can quickly become complex and challenging to comprehend, so adhering to this guideline enhances code maintainability and reduces cognitive load.

In conclusion, Pythonic coding style and conventions are at the heart of Python's philosophy. By following principles such as meaningful variable and function names, adherence to PEP 8 guidelines, and embracing constructs like list comprehensions and context managers, developers create code that is not only functional but also clear, concise, and readable. Pythonic code promotes good practices such as error handling with exceptions and using whitespace and indentation for code structuring. Overall, embracing Pythonic coding style and conventions enhances code quality and fosters a sense of unity and understanding within the Python community, making Python a language celebrated for its elegance and readability.

Writing clean, readable, and maintainable code

Clean, readable, and maintainable code is the cornerstone of software development. In Python, a language renowned for its emphasis on simplicity and readability, adhering to these principles is not only recommended but considered a best practice. Writing code that is easy to understand and maintain benefits the developer and the entire development team and the project's long-term success. This section will explore the importance of clean, readable, and maintainable code in Python and discuss strategies and practices for achieving these goals.

Clean code, as advocated by Robert C. Martin in his book "Clean Code: A Handbook of Agile Software Craftsmanship," is code that is easy to read, understand, and modify. In Python, adhering to clean code principles involves several key practices. One of the fundamental aspects is the use of meaningful and descriptive variable and function names. Choosing names that accurately convey the purpose and content of these code elements enhances code readability and eliminates the need for excessive comments or documentation.

Another crucial practice for clean code in Python is adhering to the PEP 8 style guide, which outlines code layout, naming, and organization conventions. Following PEP 8 ensures consistency across codebases and makes it easier for developers to collaborate on projects. This guide covers topics such as indentation (using spaces instead of tabs), line length limits, and naming conventions (e.g., lowercase_with_underscores for variable and function names, CamelCase for class names). Consistent code style facilitates code reviews, reduces cognitive load, and promotes readability.

Furthermore, clean code is characterized by the effective use of whitespace and indentation. Python enforces strict indentation rules, making it essential to maintain consistent and meaningful whitespace in code blocks. This practice not only contributes to the visual clarity of the code but also helps to eliminate the need for explicit block delimiters such as braces or keywords. Clean code's use of meaningful indentation is a fundamental aspect of Python's design philosophy and contributes to code's readability.

Another aspect of clean code is the avoidance of code duplication. Repeating code fragments makes the codebase larger and more challenging to maintain and increases the risk of introducing bugs when making changes. Instead of duplicating code, clean code follows the DRY (Don't Repeat Yourself) principle. Repeated functionality is encapsulated in functions or classes, making it easier to modify and maintain. By reducing duplication, clean code promotes code consistency and makes fixing issues and adding new features easier.

Additionally, clean code prioritizes using clear and informative comments and docstrings. While writing code that is self-documenting through meaningful variable and function names is essential, comments and docstrings provide additional context and explanations. Comments should focus on the "why" behind the code, explaining the rationale and purpose of specific code segments. Conversely, Docstrings provide documentation for functions, classes, and modules, allowing developers to access helpful information using tools like Python's help() function. Well-crafted comments and docstrings enhance code understanding and maintainability.

Readability is closely intertwined with clean code, as writing code that is easy to read inherently leads to code that is easy to maintain. A critical practice for improving readability is adhering to the "Zen of Python," a collection of guiding principles for writing computer programs in Python. These principles, accessible using the import this command, include aphorisms like "Readability counts" and "There should be one—and preferably only one—obvious way to do it." By embracing these principles, developers prioritize code clarity and consistency, resulting in code that is easier to work with and understand.

Another aspect of readability in Python is the use of list comprehensions and generator expressions. These concise and expressive constructs enable developers to perform operations on sequences with minimal code. List comprehensions, for example, allow developers to create new lists by applying expressions to each element of an existing list. By using these constructs, Python developers write shorter and more readable code and potentially improve performance.

Maintainability is the third pillar of writing high-quality code in Python. A maintainable codebase is one that can be modified and extended with minimal effort while preserving its functionality. Achieving maintainability involves several key practices. First and foremost is the use of modularization. Clean and maintainable Python code is organized into modular units such as functions and classes. Each module should have a single responsibility, promoting the "Single Responsibility Principle" from SOLID principles. This approach makes understanding, testing, and modifying individual components easier without affecting the entire codebase.

Additionally, maintainable code follows good practices for error handling. Exception handling with meaningful error messages ensures errors are reported accurately, allowing developers to diagnose and fix issues promptly. Well-crafted exception handling also prevents unexpected crashes and enhances the resilience of the software.

Furthermore, maintainable code is thoroughly tested. Python provides a built-in testing framework called unittest, and there are popular third-party libraries like pytest that make testing even more accessible and powerful. Writing unit tests, integration tests, and acceptance tests helps identify regressions, ensures that modifications do not break existing functionality, and aids in detecting potential issues early in the development process.

Code documentation plays a crucial role in maintainability. In addition to docstrings and comments, maintainable codebases often include high-level documentation that provides an overview of the project's architecture, design decisions, and usage guidelines. This documentation helps current developers and facilitates onboarding of new team members and eases future maintenance and updates.

In conclusion, writing clean, readable, and maintainable code in Python is essential for successful software development. Clean code adheres to principles of meaningful naming, adherence to style guides, avoiding duplication, and using whitespace and indentation for clarity. Readable code follows the Zen of Python and utilizes list comprehensions and generator expressions for brevity and expressiveness. Maintainable code is modular, handles errors gracefully, is thoroughly tested, and includes comprehensive documentation. By embracing these principles and practices, Python developers can create code that is not only functional but also easy to understand, modify, and maintain, contributing to the long-term success of their projects.

Common design patterns in Python

Design patterns are essential templates and best practices for solving recurring problems in software design and architecture. They provide a structured way of approaching common challenges and have been widely adopted by developers to improve code maintainability, flexibility, and reusability. In Python, a versatile and expressive language, many design patterns from the Gang of Four (GoF) book "Design Patterns: Elements of Reusable Object-Oriented Software" can be implemented effectively. This section will explore some of the common design patterns used in Python and discuss their applications and benefits.

The Singleton pattern ensures that a class has only one instance and provides a global access point to that instance. In Python, singletons can be implemented using a metaclass or decorators. This pattern is useful for scenarios where you need a single control point, such as managing configuration settings or database connections.

The Factory Method pattern defines an interface for creating objects but lets subclasses alter the type of objects that will be created. In Python, this pattern is often implemented using class methods or functions. It's handy when you want to delegate the responsibility of object creation to subclasses while ensuring that the client code remains decoupled from specific implementations.

The Abstract Factory pattern provides an interface for creating families of related or dependent objects without specifying their concrete classes. This pattern can be implemented in Python using a combination of classes and inheritance. It's useful when you need to ensure that a set of related objects are created together and compatible.

The Builder pattern separates the construction of a complex object from its representation, allowing you to create different representations of an object using the same construction process. In Python, this can be achieved using classes or function chaining. Builders are useful when creating complex objects with many optional components or configurations.

The Prototype pattern creates new objects by copying an existing object, known as a prototype, rather than making them from scratch. You can use the copy module or implement a custom copy method in Python. This pattern is valuable when creating objects with common characteristics but must vary slightly.

The Adapter pattern allows objects with incompatible interfaces to work together by providing a wrapper that converts one interface into another. In Python, you can implement adapters using classes or functions. It's useful when integrating with external libraries or systems with different interfaces.

The Decorator pattern attaches additional responsibilities to an object dynamically. In Python, this pattern is often used with function or class decorators. It's beneficial for adding behavior to objects without modifying their underlying code, promoting code reusability and extensibility.

The Observer pattern defines a one-to-many dependency between objects so that all its dependents are notified and updated automatically when one object changes state. In

Python, this can be achieved using built-in classes like Observable or custom implementations using the Observer pattern. It's ideal for building event-driven or publish-subscribe systems.

The Strategy pattern defines a family of interchangeable algorithms, encapsulates each one, and makes them interchangeable. In Python, you can implement strategies as classes or functions. It's valuable when you want to select an algorithm at runtime, such as choosing between different sorting algorithms based on user input.

The Command pattern encapsulates a request as an object, thereby allowing for parameterization of clients with queuing, requests, and operations. In Python, this pattern is often implemented using classes and method invocations. It's beneficial for decoupling the sender and receiver of requests, supporting undoable operations, and building command queues.

The State pattern allows an object to alter its behavior when its internal state changes. In Python, this can be achieved using classes representing different states and transitioning between them. It's useful for modeling objects with complex behavior that varies depending on their state, such as state machines.

The Composite pattern composes objects into tree structures to represent part-whole hierarchies. You can use classes and recursive data structures in Python to implement composites. It's valuable for creating complex structures from simple components and uniformly treating individual objects and compositions.

The Iterator pattern provides a way to access the elements of an aggregate object sequentially without exposing its underlying representation. In Python, iterators are an integral part of the language and can be implemented using unique methods like __iter__() and __next__(). It simplifies the traversal of collections and promotes encapsulation.

The Chain of Responsibility pattern lets you pass requests along a chain of handlers. Each handler decides to process the request or pass it to the next handler in the chain. In Python, you can implement this pattern using classes or function chaining. It's valuable for building systems where multiple objects may handle a request, and the processing order needs to be flexible.

In conclusion, design patterns are valuable tools for Python developers to solve common software design challenges effectively. These patterns promote code reusability, maintainability, and flexibility, making them essential for building robust and scalable applications. By understanding and applying these design patterns in Python, developers can create well-structured, maintainable, and adaptable codebases that meet the demands of complex software development projects.

CHAPTER X

Web Development with Python

Introduction to web frameworks like Flask and Django

Web development has evolved significantly over the years, and modern web applications require a structured and efficient approach to building and managing web resources. Web frameworks are pivotal in simplifying development by providing tools, libraries, and best practices. Flask and Django are prominent Python web frameworks offering distinctive features and catering to different web development ecosystem needs.

Flask is a lightweight and micro web framework designed for simplicity and flexibility. Created by Armin Ronacher, Flask provides a minimalistic core, allowing developers to build web applications that suit their specific requirements. Its simplicity is one of its greatest strengths, as Flask does not impose rigid structures or require specific project layouts. This flexibility makes it an excellent choice for small to medium-sized applications and prototypes.

Flask follows the WSGI (Web Server Gateway Interface) standard, which ensures compatibility with various web servers and deployment options. Developers can choose the components they need, such as database integration, template engines, and authentication, from a wide range of extensions and libraries available in the Flask ecosystem. This modular approach allows for high customization while keeping the core framework lightweight.

One of Flask's most celebrated features is its routing system. Developers can define routes and their associated view functions, making handling different HTTP methods and URL patterns easy. Flask's Jinja2 templating engine enables the creation of dynamic HTML templates, facilitating dynamic content generation. Additionally, Flask's extensive documentation and active community provide valuable resources for developers.

On the other hand, Django is a high-level web framework that prioritizes rapid development, convention over configuration, and a batteries-included approach. Developed by Adrian Holovaty and Simon Willison, Django is a full-stack framework encompassing everything needed to build complex web applications. Its primary goal is to reduce the time and effort required to create feature-rich web applications.

Django enforces a project structure and follows the "Django philosophy," which promotes the use of well-established patterns and practices. This opinionated approach means that Django provides a consistent and cohesive development experience, making it suitable for large-scale projects and teams. It includes an ORM (Object-Relational Mapping) for database access, an admin panel for content management, and a templating engine for creating dynamic web pages.

One of Django's most notable features is its authentication system, which provides robust user management out of the box. It also offers built-in support for common web development tasks such as form handling, URL routing, and database migrations. Django's middleware system also allows developers to implement cross-cutting concerns like authentication, security, and caching.

Django's architectural pattern, known as the Model-View-Controller (MVC) or Model-View-Template (MVT), divides the application into three layers: the model, which represents the data and business logic; the view, which handles user interface and presentation; and the template, which defines how data is displayed. This separation of concerns promotes maintainability and code reusability.

Both Flask and Django have strong communities, extensive documentation, and active development, making them reliable choices for web development. However, their choice depends on the project's requirements and the developer's preferences.

Flask is suitable for projects where simplicity, flexibility, and minimalism are prioritized. Developers who prefer to have complete control over the components they use and appreciate a more hands-on approach to web development often find Flask appealing. It is particularly well-suited for small to medium-sized applications, prototypes, and APIs.

On the other hand, Django excels in scenarios where rapid development, scalability, and a comprehensive set of features are essential. Projects that require built-in user authentication, admin panels, and extensive database interactions can benefit greatly from Django's batteries-included approach. Django's conventions and predefined project structure also facilitate collaboration among larger development teams.

In conclusion, Flask and Django are two popular Python web frameworks catering to different web development needs. Flask's simplicity and flexibility make it an excellent choice for small to medium-sized projects, while Django's full-stack approach and comprehensive feature set are well-suited for larger and more complex applications. The choice between these frameworks ultimately depends on the specific requirements of the project and the developer's preference for flexibility or convention. Regardless of the choice, both Flask and

Django empower developers to build robust and feature-rich web applications efficiently.

Building a simple web application

In today's digital age, web applications have become integral to our daily lives. From social media platforms to e-commerce websites, these applications have revolutionized the way we interact with the internet. Building a web application may sound daunting, but it can be a straightforward and rewarding experience with the right tools and knowledge. Python, a versatile and easy- to-learn programming language, is an excellent choice for developing web applications due to its rich ecosystem of web frameworks, such as Django and Flask. In this section, we will explore the process of building a simple web application using Python.

The first step in creating a web application with Python is to select a web framework. Two of the most popular choices are Django and Flask. Django is a high-level web framework that follows the "batteries-included" philosophy, providing a wide range of built-in features such as authentication, database management, and an admin interface. On the other hand, Flask is a micro-framework that offers more flexibility and allows developers to choose the necessary components. For the purpose of this section, we will focus on using Flask, as it provides a minimalist approach, making it an excellent choice for beginners.

Once you have chosen your web framework, setting up your development environment is the next step. Python offers a package manager called pip, which simplifies the process of installing external libraries and dependencies. You can create a virtual environment to isolate your project's dependencies and prevent conflicts with other Python projects on your system. After setting up your environment, you can install Flask using pip and start building your web application.

One of the fundamental concepts in web development is routing, which determines how URLs are mapped to functions in your application. In Flask, you can define routes using decorators. For example, the following code creates a route that responds to requests to the root URL ("/"):

```python
from flask import Flask


app = Flask(__name__)


@app.route('/')

def home():

return 'Hello, World!'


if __name__ == '__main__':

app.run()
```

In this code, we import the Flask module, create an instance of the Flask class, and use the @app.route('/') decorator to define a route for the root URL. The home() function is called when a user accesses the root URL, and it returns the text "Hello, World!" as the response. Finally, we start the Flask development server with app.run().

Web applications often require dynamic content, which means interacting with data from databases, user input, or external APIs. Flask makes it easy to handle dynamic content by allowing you to use templates to generate HTML pages. You can use the Jinja2 template engine integrated with Flask to create templates and insert dynamic data into them. For example:

```python
from flask import Flask, render_template


app = Flask(__name__)


@app.route('/')

def home():

name = 'John'

return render_template('home.html', name=name)


if __name__ == '__main__':

app.run()
```

In this code, we import the render_template function from Flask and pass a variable called name to our template, home.html. Inside the template, we can use {{ name }} to display the value of the name variable. Interacting with a database is a common requirement for many web applications. Flask makes database integration straightforward, allowing you to use various database systems, such as SQLite, PostgreSQL, or MySQL. You can use an Object-Relational Mapping (ORM) like SQLAlchemy to interact with the database in an object-oriented manner. Here's a simple example of using SQLAlchemy with Flask:

```python
from flask import Flask, render_template

from flask_sqlalchemy import SQLAlchemy
```

```python
app = Flask(__name__)

app.config['SQLALCHEMY_DATABASE_URI'] =
'sqlite:///mydatabase.db'
db = SQLAlchemy(app)


class User(db.Model):

id = db.Column(db.Integer, primary_key=True)

username = db.Column(db.String(80), unique=True,
nullable=False)


@app.route('/')

def home():

users = User.query.all()

return render_template('home.html', users=users)


if __name__ == '__main__':

app.run()
```

In this code, we create a SQLite database
called mydatabase.db and define a User model using
SQLAlchemy. The User model has two
fields: id and username. In the home() function, we
query all users from the database and pass them to the
template for rendering.

Security is a critical aspect of web development. When
building a web application, you must consider measures
to protect against common security vulnerabilities, such
as cross-site scripting (XSS), SQL injection, and cross-site
request forgery (CSRF). Flask provides built-in protection

against these vulnerabilities, but it's essential to understand and follow best practices for securing your application.

User authentication and authorization are often required for web applications with restricted areas or user-specific content. Flask-Login and Flask-Principal are popular extensions that can help you implement user authentication and access control in your application. With these extensions, you can create user login systems, manage user sessions, and control access to different parts of your application.

Deployment is the final step in bringing your web application to the public. You can choose from various hosting providers and platforms, such as Heroku, AWS, or a traditional web hosting service. Flask applications are typically deployed using WSGI servers like Gunicorn or uWSGI, which bridge your application and the web server. You'll need to configure your server, set up a domain name, and ensure your application is secure and ready for production use.

In conclusion, building a simple web application with Python using the Flask web framework is achievable, even for beginners. Flask lets you quickly set up routes, handle dynamic content, interact with databases, and secure your application. By following best practices and continuously learning, you can create web applications that cater to your specific needs and provide valuable experiences to users. Whether you're building a personal blog, an e-commerce site, or a web-based tool, Python and Flask offer a solid foundation for your web development journey.

Deploying Python web applications

In the world of web development, creating a Python web application is just the beginning of the journey. Once you've built your application, the next crucial step is deploying it to a server so that it can be accessed by users worldwide. Deploying a Python web application involves a series of steps that ensure your application is live, stable, and ready for production use. In this section, we will explore the process of deploying Python web applications, covering essential aspects such as server selection, web server configuration, application deployment, and scaling considerations.

Selecting the correct server for hosting your Python web application is the first and fundamental decision you must make. There are several hosting options available, each with its advantages and limitations. One common choice is to use cloud hosting providers like Amazon Web Services (AWS), Google Cloud Platform (GCP), or Microsoft Azure. These platforms offer scalability, reliability, and various services to support your application's infrastructure needs. Another option is traditional web hosting providers that offer shared hosting, virtual private servers (VPS), or dedicated servers. The choice depends on your project's requirements, budget, and technical expertise.

Once you've chosen a hosting provider, the next step is to configure a web server. A web server is a software responsible for handling incoming HTTP requests and serving your Python application to users. Two popular choices for deploying Python web applications are Gunicorn (Green Unicorn) and uWSGI. These WSGI (Web Server Gateway Interface) servers are designed to work seamlessly with Python web frameworks like Flask and Django. To configure a web server, you typically need to specify the host and port where your application will listen for incoming requests and provide information about your application, such as the location of your Python script and application entry point.

After configuring your web server, you must deploy your Python web application to the server. This involves transferring your application's code, dependencies, and static files to the server's file system. You can use tools like SCP (Secure Copy Protocol) or SFTP (Secure File Transfer Protocol) to manually upload your application to the server, or you can leverage deployment automation tools like Ansible, Fabric, or Docker to streamline the process. It's crucial to ensure that your application's dependencies are correctly installed on the server and that you have set up the appropriate environment variables or configuration files for your application to run smoothly in the production environment.

Web applications often rely on databases to store and retrieve data. When deploying your Python web application, you must consider how to manage your database. You can choose to host your database on the same server as your application, but for scalability and separation of concerns, it's often recommended to use managed database services provided by your hosting provider. These services handle database administration tasks such as backups, replication, and scaling, allowing you to focus on your application code. Popular databases for Python web applications include PostgreSQL, MySQL, and MongoDB, each with its strengths and use cases.

To ensure the reliability and availability of your deployed Python web application, you should consider implementing load balancing and redundancy strategies. Load balancing distributes incoming traffic across multiple server instances, preventing any single server from becoming a bottleneck. Redundancy involves deploying numerous instances of your application in different regions or availability zones to mitigate the risk of downtime due to server failures or network issues. Cloud hosting providers often offer load balancing and redundancy solutions, which can be configured to meet your application's needs.

Monitoring and performance optimization are ongoing tasks when deploying Python web applications. Monitoring tools like New Relic, Datadog, or Prometheus can help you track server performance, identify bottlenecks, and troubleshoot issues. You can make informed decisions about optimizing your application's code and infrastructure by analyzing server logs, error logs, and performance metrics. Performance optimization techniques include caching, database indexing, code profiling, and code minification.

In conclusion, deploying a Python web application is a critical phase in the development process that requires careful planning and consideration of various factors. Selecting the right hosting provider, configuring a web server, and deploying your application are essential steps to ensure your application is live and accessible to users. Additionally, managing databases, implementing load balancing and redundancy, and continuously monitoring and optimizing your application are crucial for maintaining its reliability and performance. Deploying Python web applications may seem complex, but with the proper knowledge and tools, it can be a manageable and rewarding experience, allowing you to share your creations with the world and provide valuable services to your users.

CHAPTER XI

Data Analysis and Visualization

Working with data using libraries like Pandas and NumPy

In data manipulation and analysis, the Python programming language shines brightly thanks to the robust libraries available for handling data efficiently. Two of the most prominent libraries in this domain are Pandas and NumPy. These libraries empower data scientists, analysts, and developers to work with data seamlessly, from data cleaning and preparation to complex statistical analysis and visualization. In this section, we will explore how Pandas and NumPy contribute to the field of data science and why they are indispensable tools in the toolkit of anyone dealing with data.

Pandas, short for "Panel Data," is a high-level data manipulation library providing data structures and functions for structured data. At its core, Pandas introduces two primary data structures: the DataFrame and the Series. A DataFrame is a two-dimensional, tabular data structure, resembling a spreadsheet or a SQL table, where data is organized in rows and columns. Conversely, a Series is a one-dimensional labeled array that can hold various data types. These data structures are the foundation upon which Pandas builds its extensive set of data manipulation capabilities.

Pandas excels in data cleaning and preparation. It offers various functions for handling missing data, duplicate values, and outliers. You can filter, transform, and aggregate data effortlessly, making it ideal for tasks like data cleansing, data normalization, and feature engineering. The ability to easily merge, join, and pivot data tables simplifies complex data transformations, enabling you to extract meaningful insights from raw data effectively.

NumPy, short for "Numerical Python," is a fundamental library for numerical and scientific computing in Python. It introduces a powerful multi-dimensional array object called ndarray, which is at the heart of most numerical computations performed in Python. NumPy provides efficient and vectorized operations on arrays, making it an essential library for numerical tasks such as linear algebra, calculus, and statistical analysis.

One of NumPy's strengths lies in its ability to perform element-wise operations on arrays, eliminating the need for explicit loops in many calculations. This feature improves the efficiency of numerical computations and makes the code more readable and concise. Additionally, NumPy offers a rich set of mathematical functions and random number generators, further enhancing its utility for scientific computing.

Pandas and NumPy complement each other seamlessly, creating a potent ecosystem for data analysis. Pandas Series and DataFrames are built on top of NumPy arrays, allowing you to leverage NumPy's array operations within Pandas. This integration simplifies data manipulation tasks involving structured data and numerical computations. For instance, you can use NumPy functions to perform element-wise operations on Pandas Series, enhancing the flexibility and performance of your data analysis code.

Data visualization is a crucial aspect of data analysis, as it helps communicate findings and insights effectively. While Pandas and NumPy excel at data manipulation and numerical computations, libraries like Matplotlib and

Seaborn are often used in conjunction to create informative plots and charts. These visualization libraries integrate seamlessly with Pandas DataFrames, enabling you to generate a wide range of charts, including bar plots, scatter plots, histograms, and heatmaps, to showcase your data and results.

When working with large datasets, memory efficiency becomes a concern. Both Pandas and NumPy provide mechanisms to optimize memory usage. For example, Pandas allows you to specify data types (e.g., int, float) that consume less memory, while NumPy provides methods to control memory allocation and alignment for arrays. These optimizations are especially valuable when dealing with big data or when running data analysis on resource-constrained environments.

In conclusion, Pandas and NumPy are indispensable tools in the world of data science and analysis. Pandas excels in data manipulation and preparation, providing a rich set of functions for cleaning, transforming, and aggregating data. Conversely, NumPy empowers numerical and scientific computing by introducing efficient multi-dimensional arrays and vectorized operations. The seamless integration between Pandas and NumPy simplifies complex data analysis tasks, allowing data scientists and analysts to efficiently derive meaningful insights from data. When combined with visualization libraries like Matplotlib and Seaborn, these libraries offer a comprehensive toolkit for data professionals to explore, analyze, and communicate their findings effectively. Whether you are a data scientist, analyst, or developer, mastering Pandas and NumPy is a valuable investment that will enhance your ability to work with data and uncover hidden patterns and insights within it.

Creating data visualizations with Matplotlib and Seaborn

Data visualization is an essential aspect of data analysis and communication. It enables us to make sense of complex data sets, identify trends, and convey insights effectively to a wide audience. Among the various data visualization libraries available for Python, Matplotlib and Seaborn stand out as two powerful and versatile tools that allow data scientists, analysts, and researchers to create compelling and informative visualizations. In this section, we will explore the capabilities of Matplotlib and Seaborn, highlighting their strengths and explaining how they can be employed to create meaningful data visualizations.

Matplotlib, often referred to as the foundational library for data visualization in Python, provides a comprehensive set of tools for creating static, animated, and interactive visualizations. It offers a wide range of chart types, including line plots, scatter plots, bar plots, histograms, pie charts, and more. Matplotlib's flexibility allows you to customize nearly every aspect of your visualizations, from colors and markers to fonts and annotations. This level of customization makes it an ideal choice when you need fine-grained control over your plots to tailor them to specific requirements.

Matplotlib operates on a low level, which means it offers precise control over individual chart components. You can create a figure and one or more axes (subplots) and then add various elements like data points, lines, and text to these axes. While this approach gives you immense control, it can also be more verbose, especially for simple plots. However, Matplotlib's object-oriented API makes modifying and enhancing your visualizations straightforward.

Seaborn, on the other hand, is a high-level data visualization library built on top of Matplotlib. It is designed to simplify the creation of attractive and informative statistical plots. Seaborn comes with built-in themes and color palettes that improve the aesthetics of your visualizations and make it easy to create professional-looking plots. Additionally, Seaborn provides functions for creating complex visualizations like heatmaps, pair plots, and violin plots with minimal code, which can be particularly beneficial for exploratory data analysis.

One of Seaborn's key strengths is its ability to work seamlessly with Pandas DataFrames. You can pass a DataFrame directly to a Seaborn plotting function, automatically extracting and visualizing the data. This tight integration simplifies the data preparation process, allowing you to focus on the visualization itself. Seaborn also excels in producing informative statistical visualizations, such as box plots and regression plots, which can be crucial for understanding relationships and trends within your data.

Both Matplotlib and Seaborn offer various ways to customize the appearance of your visualizations. You can adjust colors, markers, and line styles, add titles and labels, modify axis scales, and incorporate annotations to enhance the readability and clarity of your plots. Matplotlib's low-level approach provides ultimate control over these aspects, but Seaborn's high-level functions often provide sensible defaults, which can save time while still delivering visually appealing results.

In terms of interactivity, Matplotlib can be extended using interactive visualization libraries like Plotly or Bokeh to create interactive dashboards and web applications. Seaborn, on the other hand, primarily focuses on static visualizations. However, it's worth noting that both libraries complement each other, and you can use Matplotlib for customized interactive visualizations alongside Seaborn for its simplicity in creating static plots.

When choosing between Matplotlib and Seaborn, it's essential to consider the specific requirements of your data visualization task. Matplotlib's versatility and fine-grained control make it an excellent choice for creating highly customized plots, especially when your visualizations must adhere to strict design guidelines. On the other hand, Seaborn is well-suited for tasks that involve quickly generating aesthetically pleasing and informative plots, making it a valuable tool for exploratory data analysis and rapid visualization prototyping.

In conclusion, Matplotlib and Seaborn are indispensable tools in the world of data visualization, catering to different needs and preferences of data professionals. Matplotlib's flexibility and precision allow for intricate customization, making it the go-to choice for highly tailored plots. On the other hand, Seaborn simplifies the creation of visually appealing statistical visualizations and seamlessly integrates with Pandas DataFrames, streamlining the data visualization process. Whether you are a data scientist, analyst, or researcher, mastering these libraries will enable you to convey your insights effectively and engage your audience through compelling and informative data visualizations. By leveraging the strengths of Matplotlib and Seaborn, you can unlock your data's full potential and present it visually compellingly, enhancing understanding and decision-making.

Analyzing real-world datasets

Analyzing real-world datasets in Python has become indispensable in today's data-driven world. Python, with its rich ecosystem of libraries and tools, offers a versatile and potent environment for data analysis tasks. From business data to scientific research and beyond, Python provides the means to extract insights, make data-driven decisions, and gain a deeper understanding of real-world datasets' complex patterns and trends.

Data acquisition is one of the first steps in analyzing real-world datasets in Python. Python offers various methods and libraries for collecting data from diverse sources. Whether you need to scrape data from websites using libraries like Beautiful Soup or requests, access data from databases using SQLAlchemy, or fetch data from APIs using packages like requests or the popular requests library, Python provides the tools to fetch data from the web, databases, or external sources efficiently. This initial phase sets the foundation for the analysis and requires a deep understanding of the data's source and structure.

Once the data is acquired, data cleaning and preprocessing become paramount. Real-world datasets are seldom perfect and often contain missing values, outliers, duplicates, or inconsistencies. Python's data manipulation libraries, such as Pandas, offer extensive data cleaning and preprocessing functionality. Pandas enable you to clean the data by handling missing values, removing duplicates, and addressing outliers. Moreover, it provides powerful data transformation and aggregation capabilities, allowing you to reshape and structure the data to suit the requirements of your analysis.

Exploratory data analysis (EDA) is critical in analyzing real-world datasets. EDA involves techniques and tools for understanding the data's underlying patterns and characteristics. Python's libraries, such as Pandas for data manipulation and Matplotlib and Seaborn for data visualization, play a pivotal role in this phase. Descriptive statistics, data visualizations, and data summaries help reveal the dataset's trends, relationships, and potential outliers. EDA is an iterative process that informs further data cleaning and preprocessing steps and guides the direction of the analysis.

Feature selection and engineering are essential steps in preparing real-world datasets for analysis. These processes involve selecting the most relevant variables (features) and creating new features that may enhance the dataset's analytical power. Python's libraries provide various techniques for feature selection and engineering. For example, Scikit-learn offers tools for feature selection based on statistical tests and feature importance scores from machine learning models. Additionally, domain knowledge often plays a crucial role in identifying which features are most informative for a particular analysis.

Depending on the specific analysis goals, Python offers a wide range of analytical approaches for real-world datasets. Statistical methods, machine learning algorithms, and deep learning models can be applied to perform tasks such as regression, classification, clustering, and anomaly detection. Libraries like Scikit-learn and TensorFlow provide comprehensive support for these tasks, making it accessible to both data scientists and analysts. Choosing the appropriate analysis method is crucial and depends on the problem statement and the nature of the data.

Validation and evaluation of the analysis are paramount to ensure the reliability and generalizability of the results. Cross-validation techniques, such as k-fold cross-validation, allow you to estimate how well your model or analysis performs on unseen data. Python libraries like Scikit-learn provide built-in functions for conducting cross-validation and evaluating models. Selecting appropriate evaluation metrics, such as accuracy, precision, recall, or mean squared error, depends on the specific analysis and its goals. Proper validation and evaluation help validate the analysis's robustness and provide confidence in the results.

The final step in analyzing real-world datasets in Python is the communication of findings. Effectively conveying insights and results to stakeholders, colleagues, or decision-makers is essential. Python's data visualization libraries, including Matplotlib, Seaborn, and Plotly, are vital in creating informative and visually appealing charts, graphs, and plots. These visualizations help tell a compelling story about the data and its implications. Furthermore, generating clear and concise reports, presentations, or interactive dashboards aids in conveying the significance of the analysis and guiding informed decision-making.

In conclusion, Python has firmly established itself as a go-to tool for analyzing real-world datasets across various domains. The robust ecosystem of libraries and tools, including Pandas, Matplotlib, Seaborn, Scikit-learn, and more, provides a powerful and versatile environment for data professionals. From data acquisition and cleaning to exploratory data analysis, feature engineering, modeling, validation, and communication of findings, Python offers a comprehensive toolkit to tackle the complexities of real-world datasets. As data continues to grow in volume and importance, the ability to analyze real-world datasets in Python remains a crucial skill for data scientists, analysts, and researchers who seek to extract valuable insights and make data-driven decisions in an increasingly data-centric world.

CHAPTER XII

Machine Learning and AI with Python

Introduction to machine learning and AI concepts

Machine learning and artificial intelligence (AI) have become ubiquitous technologies in our digital age, reshaping industries, enabling new capabilities, and enhancing decision-making processes. At the heart of these innovations lies the Python programming language, which has emerged as the preferred choice for developing machine learning and AI applications. In this section, we will explore the fundamentals of machine learning and AI concepts, and how Python is a powerful tool for their implementation and application.

Machine learning is a subset of AI that focuses on developing algorithms and models that enable computer systems to improve their performance on a specific task through experience and data. The central idea is to train a model using historical data so that it can make predictions, classify objects, or discover patterns in new, unseen data. With its extensive libraries and frameworks, Python provides a comprehensive ecosystem for machine learning tasks.

One of the fundamental concepts in machine learning is supervised learning. In supervised learning, a model is trained on a labeled dataset, where the input data is associated with corresponding target values or labels. Python libraries like Scikit-learn offer a wide range of supervised learning algorithms, including linear regression for regression tasks, decision trees, and support vector machines for classification tasks. These algorithms can be easily implemented and applied to real-world problems in Python.

Another essential concept is unsupervised learning, which aims to discover patterns or structures in the data without explicit labels. Clustering and dimensionality reduction are common tasks in unsupervised learning. Python's Scikit-learn provides algorithms for clustering, such as k-means, and for dimensionality reduction, such as principal component analysis (PCA). These techniques are valuable for data exploration, feature extraction, and grouping similar data points together.

Deep learning is a subset of machine learning that focuses on artificial neural networks inspired by the human brain's structure. Deep learning models, often implemented using Python libraries like TensorFlow and PyTorch, have gained immense popularity due to their ability to excel in tasks like image recognition, natural language processing, and speech recognition. Convolutional neural networks (CNNs) and recurrent neural networks (RNNs) are common architectures used in deep learning.

Reinforcement learning is a branch of machine learning where agents learn to make decisions by interacting with an environment and receiving feedback in the form of rewards or penalties. Python's libraries, such as OpenAI's Gym, provide environments for reinforcement learning experiments. Reinforcement learning algorithms like Q-learning and deep reinforcement learning methods, including Deep Q-Networks (DQNs), have been used to train agents in various applications, from game-playing to robotics.

Python's ecosystem for machine learning is not limited to libraries and frameworks alone; it also includes rich data preprocessing, visualization, and evaluation tools. Libraries like Pandas offer data manipulation capabilities, while Matplotlib and Seaborn enable data visualization. Scikit-learn provides functions for model evaluation, cross-validation, and hyperparameter tuning, allowing data scientists and machine learning practitioners to build, assess, and optimize models efficiently.

Artificial intelligence (AI) extends beyond machine learning and encompasses various techniques and applications. AI aims to create intelligent agents or systems that can perceive their environment, reason, learn, and make decisions autonomously. In Python, AI concepts are applied in areas such as natural language processing (NLP), computer vision, robotics, and expert systems.

Natural language processing (NLP) is a subfield of AI that focuses on the interaction between computers and human languages. Python's libraries, such as NLTK and spaCy, offer tools for text processing, sentiment analysis, and named entity recognition. Pretrained language models like BERT and GPT-3, accessible through Python interfaces, have revolutionized NLP tasks, enabling machines to understand and generate human-like text.

Computer vision is another AI field that aims to teach machines to interpret visual information from the world, often involving tasks like image classification, object detection, and image segmentation. Python's OpenCV library provides a comprehensive suite of tools for computer vision tasks. Deep learning frameworks like TensorFlow and PyTorch have also been instrumental in advancing computer vision capabilities through architectures like CNNs.

Robotics is a domain where AI and machine learning converge to enable machines to interact with the physical world. Python libraries like ROS (Robot Operating System) provide a platform for developing and controlling robots. Machine learning techniques are employed in robotics for tasks such as autonomous navigation, object manipulation, and robot perception.

Expert systems are AI applications that mimic human expertise in a specific domain. Python's symbolic reasoning libraries, like SymPy and Pyke, enable developing expert systems for tasks like medical diagnosis, financial analysis, and decision support. These systems use rule-based logic and knowledge representation to provide expert-level recommendations and insights.

In conclusion, Python has emerged as a prominent programming language for exploring and implementing machine learning and AI concepts. Its rich ecosystem of libraries, frameworks, and tools makes it a versatile choice for data analysis, modeling, and AI development. Whether you are interested in predictive modeling, computer vision, natural language processing, or robotics, Python offers the resources and flexibility to experiment, innovate, and apply AI and machine learning to real-world problems. As AI and machine learning continue to evolve, Python's role as a powerful platform for these technologies remains instrumental in shaping our increasingly intelligent and automated world.

Using libraries like Scikit-Learn and TensorFlow

Python, with its extensive ecosystem of libraries and frameworks, has become the go-to language for machine learning and deep learning tasks. Among the myriad of tools available, Scikit-Learn and TensorFlow stand out as two of the most influential libraries for data scientists, researchers, and developers in artificial intelligence (AI) and machine learning. In this section, we will explore the capabilities and applications of Scikit-Learn and TensorFlow, highlighting how they are used with Python to tackle various machine learning and deep learning challenges.

Scikit-Learn, often abbreviated as sklearn, is a versatile machine-learning library that simplifies the implementation of common machine-learning algorithms. It provides a unified interface for various supervised and unsupervised learning tasks, making it an ideal choice for newcomers to the field and seasoned practitioners alike. Scikit-Learn includes a wide range of algorithms for classification, regression, clustering, dimensionality reduction, and more. These algorithms cover a spectrum of techniques, from simple linear models to complex ensemble methods and support vector machines.

One of Scikit-Learn's strengths is its user-friendly and consistent API. It follows a straightforward "fit-transform-predict" paradigm, allowing users to quickly build and train models, transform data, and make predictions with minimal effort. This simplicity enables data scientists to experiment with different algorithms and approaches efficiently. Additionally, Scikit-Learn provides extensive documentation and practical examples, making it accessible to users of all levels of expertise.

Scikit-Learn's vast array of preprocessing tools and utilities are indispensable for data preparation and feature engineering. It offers data scaling, feature selection, dimensionality reduction, and imputation techniques, helping users clean and preprocess data effectively. Furthermore, Scikit-Learn facilitates model evaluation and hyperparameter tuning through cross-validation, grid search, and scoring metrics, ensuring that models are robust and optimized for the task at hand.

TensorFlow, developed by Google, is an open-source deep learning framework that has recently gained immense popularity. It is designed to build and train artificial neural networks for various AI and machine learning applications. TensorFlow's flexibility and scalability make it suitable for various tasks, from image and speech recognition to natural language processing and reinforcement learning. TensorFlow's architecture is based on a computational graph, allowing users to define and optimize complex neural network structures easily.

Deep learning, a subfield of machine learning that focuses on neural networks with multiple layers, has been revolutionized by TensorFlow. TensorFlow offers a high-level API called Keras, which simplifies the creation and training of deep neural networks. Keras's user-friendly interface and abstraction of complex operations have made it a preferred choice for many deep learning practitioners. TensorFlow also provides low-level APIs that allow users to customize neural network architectures and control every aspect of the training process.

One of TensorFlow's key features is its CPU and GPU acceleration support. This capability enables users to train deep learning models on powerful graphics processing units, significantly reducing training times and making complex tasks feasible. TensorFlow's distributed computing capabilities further enhance its scalability, allowing users to train models on clusters of machines for large-scale AI and machine learning projects.

The TensorFlow ecosystem includes various add-on libraries and tools that extend its functionality. For example, TensorFlow Serving enables users to deploy trained models as production-ready APIs, while TensorFlow Lite allows models to be deployed on mobile and edge devices. Additionally, TensorFlow's integration with TensorBoard, a visualization tool, makes monitoring and debug deep learning experiments easier, providing insights into the model's performance and behavior.

The decision to use Scikit-Learn or TensorFlow depends on the specific task, the complexity of the problem, and the user's familiarity with each library. Scikit-Learn is an excellent choice for classical machine learning tasks, especially when dealing with structured data, feature engineering, and model evaluation. It provides a gentle learning curve and a wide range of algorithms suitable for most applications. Conversely, TensorFlow shines in deep learning and neural network-based tasks, such as image and speech recognition or natural language processing. It offers the flexibility needed to design and train complex neural architectures while harnessing the power of GPUs for efficient training.

In conclusion, Scikit-Learn and TensorFlow are powerful libraries that empower Python users to tackle various machine learning and deep learning challenges. Scikit-Learn simplifies the implementation of traditional machine learning algorithms, making it accessible and efficient for data scientists and analysts. TensorFlow, with its focus on deep learning and neural networks, has transformed the field of AI and enables users to create sophisticated models for complex tasks. As Python continues to dominate the field of machine learning and AI, the combination of Scikit-Learn and TensorFlow provides a robust and versatile toolkit for researchers, developers, and data professionals seeking to push the boundaries of artificial intelligence and machine learning.

Building a simple machine learning model

Machine learning has become an integral part of many industries, from healthcare to finance, and Python has emerged as the language of choice for developing machine learning models due to its versatility and a vast array of libraries and tools. In this section, we will delve into the process of building a simple machine learning model using Python, highlighting the fundamental steps and key concepts involved in the journey of transforming data into actionable insights.

Data acquisition and preprocessing is the first step in building a machine learning model. High-quality data is the foundation for any successful machine learning model. This process involves gathering, cleaning, and preparing the data for analysis. Python's libraries, such as

Pandas, facilitate data manipulation and transformation. Missing values are handled, outliers are addressed, and the data is structured in a way that is suitable for the chosen machine learning algorithm. This crucial phase ensures that the data accurately represents the problem at hand.

Once the data is ready, feature selection and engineering are the next steps. Features are the variables or attributes the model uses to make predictions or classifications. Feature selection involves choosing the most relevant features while discarding irrelevant or redundant ones. Feature engineering may include creating or transforming new features to capture valuable information. Python offers a wide range of feature selection and engineering tools, including Scikit-Learn and Feature-Engine, which simplify these tasks.

Selecting an appropriate machine learning algorithm is a critical decision in the model-building process. Python's Scikit-Learn library provides many machine learning algorithms, including regression, classification, clustering, and more. The choice of algorithm depends on the nature of the problem. For example, linear regression is suitable for predicting continuous values, while decision trees are effective for classification tasks. Python's consistent API in Scikit-Learn makes it easy to experiment with different algorithms and determine which one best fits the data and problem domain.

Once the algorithm is chosen, the data is split into training and testing sets to evaluate the model's performance. The training set is used to teach the model to make predictions, while the testing set is used to assess its accuracy on unseen data. Python provides functions and libraries for splitting the data, including Scikit-Learn's train-test-split function. Proper evaluation metrics, such as accuracy, precision, recall, and F1-score, are chosen depending on the type of problem (classification or regression) and the domain.

Training the machine learning model involves feeding it with the training data and adjusting its internal parameters to learn from the patterns and relationships within the data. Python libraries like Scikit-Learn offer easy-to-use functions for training models, allowing data scientists to efficiently build and fine-tune their models. The training process often involves hyperparameter tuning, where different combinations of hyperparameters are tested to find the optimal configuration that maximizes the model's performance.

The trained model is then used to predict or classify new, unseen data. Python's libraries, such as Scikit-Learn, provide simple interfaces for making predictions with the trained model. Depending on the application, the model's predictions can be used to gain insights, make decisions, or automate tasks. Python's versatility enables data scientists to integrate machine learning models seamlessly into various workflows, from web applications to data pipelines.

Regular model evaluation and monitoring are crucial for maintaining the model's performance over time. Python libraries like Scikit-Learn provide tools for cross-validation, which helps assess how well the model is likely to generalize to new data. Regular retraining of the model with fresh data can also help prevent model degradation. Additionally, monitoring the model's predictions and performance in a production environment is essential to identify any issues or changes in data distribution.

In conclusion, building a simple machine learning model with Python involves several key steps, including data acquisition and preprocessing, feature selection and engineering, algorithm selection, model training, evaluation, and deployment. Python's extensive libraries and tools simplify each of these stages, making it an ideal choice for data scientists and machine learning practitioners. As machine learning continues to play an increasingly prominent role in solving real-world problems, Python's flexibility and ease of use make it a valuable asset for those looking to harness the power of data and transform it into actionable insights through machine learning models.

CONCLUSION

"Python Unleashed: Mastering the Art of Efficient Coding" is a remarkable journey through the world of Python programming, offering readers an in-depth understanding of the language and its capabilities. As we conclude our exploration of this book, it becomes evident that it is a valuable resource for both beginners and experienced programmers.

One of the standout features of this book is its ability to cater to a broad audience. Whether you are a novice looking to start your programming journey or an experienced developer seeking to enhance your Python skills, "Python Unleashed" provides a comprehensive and structured approach. The author's clear and concise explanations and numerous practical examples ensure that readers of all skill levels can grasp the concepts and apply them effectively.

Efficiency is a recurring theme throughout the book, and rightly so. Python is renowned for its simplicity and readability, but it is also known for its power and versatility. "Python Unleashed" does an excellent job of teaching readers how to harness the full potential of Python, enabling them to write efficient and elegant code. From optimization techniques to best practices, this book equips programmers with the knowledge and tools needed to write code that not only works but works efficiently.

One of the book's strong points is its focus on real-world applications. It goes beyond teaching the language's syntax and dives into practical use cases. Readers are introduced to various Python libraries and frameworks, including NumPy, pandas, and Django, which are essential in today's data science, web development, and automation projects. This practical approach ensures that readers can immediately apply what they learn to their own projects.

Furthermore, "Python Unleashed" emphasizes the importance of good coding practices and software design. It guides readers through clean code principles, code maintainability, and collaboration with other developers. These skills are invaluable, especially for those aiming to work in professional software development environments.

In conclusion, "Python Unleashed: Mastering the Art of Efficient Coding" is a comprehensive and accessible resource for anyone looking to master Python programming. Its focus on efficiency, real-world applications, and good coding practices equips readers with the skills and knowledge necessary to become proficient Python developers. Whether you are a beginner or an experienced coder, this book is a valuable addition to your Python library and a stepping stone to becoming a more skilled and efficient programmer.

Thank you for buying and reading/ listening to our book. If you found this book useful/ helpful please take a few minutes and leave a review on the platform where you purchased our book. Your feedback matters greatly to us.